CW01301499

Palgrave Studies in Victims and Victimology

Series Editors
Pamela Davies, Department of Social Sciences,
Northumbria University, Newcastle upon Tyne, UK
Tyrone Kirchengast, Law School, University of Sydney,
Sydney, NSW, Australia

In recent decades, a growing emphasis on meeting the needs and rights of victims of crime in criminal justice policy and practice has fuelled the development of research, theory, policy and practice outcomes stretching across the globe. This growth of interest in the victim of crime has seen victimology move from being a distinct subset of criminology in academia to a specialist area of study and research in its own right. *Palgrave Studies in Victims and Victimology* showcases the work of contemporary scholars of victimological research and publishes some of the highest-quality research in the field. The series reflects the range and depth of research and scholarship in this burgeoning area, combining contributions from both established scholars who have helped to shape the field and more recent entrants. It also reflects both the global nature of many of the issues surrounding justice for victims of crime and social harm and the international span of scholarship researching and writing about them.

Editorial Board
Antony Pemberton, Tilburg University, Netherlands
Jo-Anne Wemmers, Montreal University, Canada
Joanna Shapland, Sheffield University, UK
Jonathan Doak, Durham University, UK

Tom Daems · Elien Goossens
Editors

Understanding Prisoner Victimisation

palgrave
macmillan

Editors
Tom Daems
Leuven Institute of Criminology (LINC)
KU Leuven
Leuven, Belgium

Elien Goossens
Leuven Institute of Criminology (LINC)
KU Leuven
Leuven, Belgium

ISSN 2947-9355   ISSN 2947-9363 (electronic)
Palgrave Studies in Victims and Victimology
ISBN 978-3-031-54349-4   ISBN 978-3-031-54350-0 (eBook)
https://doi.org/10.1007/978-3-031-54350-0

© The Editor(s) (if applicable) and The Author(s), under exclusive license to Springer Nature Switzerland AG 2024

This work is subject to copyright. All rights are solely and exclusively licensed by the Publisher, whether the whole or part of the material is concerned, specifically the rights of translation, reprinting, reuse of illustrations, recitation, broadcasting, reproduction on microfilms or in any other physical way, and transmission or information storage and retrieval, electronic adaptation, computer software, or by similar or dissimilar methodology now known or hereafter developed.
The use of general descriptive names, registered names, trademarks, service marks, etc. in this publication does not imply, even in the absence of a specific statement, that such names are exempt from the relevant protective laws and regulations and therefore free for general use.
The publisher, the authors and the editors are safe to assume that the advice and information in this book are believed to be true and accurate at the date of publication. Neither the publisher nor the authors or the editors give a warranty, expressed or implied, with respect to the material contained herein or for any errors or omissions that may have been made. The publisher remains neutral with regard to jurisdictional claims in published maps and institutional affiliations.

Cover illustration: Alena Ivochkina/Alamy Stock Photo

This Palgrave Macmillan imprint is published by the registered company Springer Nature Switzerland AG
The registered company address is: Gewerbestrasse 11, 6330 Cham, Switzerland

Paper in this product is recyclable.

Preface

The term 'victimology' was first coined by Benjamin Mendelsohn in 1946. Initially, however, victimology had little interest in the fate of the victim: from an aetiological point of view, the first victimologists were predominantly interested in better understanding the origins of crime by studying the role the victim might play in it. Marvin Wolfgang, for example, introduced the term 'victim precipitation' with which he aimed to objectify the discussion on the role of the victim and to move away from a moralising and legal discourse aimed at establishing responsibility for crime.

From the 1970s onwards, victimology increasingly began to distance itself from such aetiological questions and the experiences of victims moved to the centre of debate and research: what is the incidence of victimisation? What are the consequences? What are the risks? What about repeat victimisation? How can we prevent (re)victimisation? How can the police, judiciary, welfare better respond to victims' needs? What rights for victims? What about reparation and restorative justice? However, prisoners *as victims* usually remained out of the picture of victimology. This is hardly surprising: people convicted of crime are mainly seen as perpetrators, not as victims of crime. In the meantime, however, we know that a lot of victimisation also takes place behind bars. Those unusual or non-'ideal' victims are at the centre of this volume on understanding prisoner victimisation.

The idea for this book grew out of an international workshop 'Understanding prisoner victimisation', which was organised on 8 June 2023 at KU Leuven, Belgium. In that workshop we presented the main findings of the FWO project 'Victimisation in detention: prevalence, causes and consequences' (project n° G079219N). In order to broaden the discussion and to introduce work from other parts of Europe we invited scholars involved in empirical research from England and Wales and the Netherlands, and we included further reflections on methodology, concepts and prison monitoring.

We are grateful to FWO for providing generous funding for the project and to the Research Council of KU Leuven to grant us a brief extension through its COVID-19 emergency fund. We also would like to thank all authors and participants in our Leuven workshop and Josie Taylor and her team at Palgrave Macmillan for help and support when preparing the manuscript.

Leuven, Belgium
December 2023

Tom Daems
Elien Goossens

Contents

Why Should We Study Prisoner Victimisation?   1
Tom Daems and Elien Goossens

Who's Who? Individual Characteristics of Those Involved in Sexual Assaults in Adult Men's Prisons in England and Wales   13
Jo Wilkinson

Mapping and Explaining Victimisation Among Prisoners in Flanders   49
Elien Goossens and Tom Daems

The Victim-Offender Overlap in Prisons and Associated Challenges for Prison Managers   89
Esther F. J. C. van Ginneken

Vulnerability and Victimhood in Prison: Reflecting on the Concept of Vulnerability in Prisoner Victimisation Research   115
Aurore Vanliefde

Methodological Challenges in Victimisation Studies 143
Elien Goossens

Independent Monitoring and Victimisation in Prisons 175
Tom Daems

Index 185

Contributors

Tom Daems Leuven Institute of Criminology (LINC), KU Leuven, Leuven, Belgium

Elien Goossens Leuven Institute of Criminology (LINC), KU Leuven, Leuven, Belgium

Esther F. J. C. van Ginneken Institute for Criminal Law and Criminology, Leiden University, Leiden, The Netherlands

Aurore Vanliefde Faculty of Law and Criminology, KU Leuven, Leuven, Belgium

Jo Wilkinson University of Southampton, Southampton, UK; College of Policing, Coventry, UK

List of Figures

Who's Who? Individual Characteristics of Those Involved in Sexual Assaults in Adult Men's Prisons in England and Wales

Fig. 1   Criminal offence type (grouped) of victims and perpetrators   29

Methodological Challenges in Victimisation Studies

Fig. 1   Percentage of missing data across independent items in the 'Detention monitor', N = 927 (Goossens & Daems' study, this volume)   165

List of Tables

Who's Who? Individual Characteristics of Those Involved in Sexual Assaults in Adult Men's Prisons in England and Wales

Table 1	Type of sexual assault by role/involvement	22
Table 2	Time since reception in current prison at the time of the reported sexual assault (perpetrators and victims only)	25
Table 3	Ethnicity (grouped) of victims and perpetrators	34

Mapping and Explaining Victimisation Among Prisoners in Flanders

Table 1	Frequencies and prevalence rates of emotional victimisation (N = 884)	63
Table 2	Frequencies and prevalence rates of material victimisation (N = 896)	65
Table 3	Frequencies and prevalence rates of physical victimisation (N = 901)	66

Table 4	Frequencies and prevalence rates of sexual victimisation (N = 897)	67
Table 5	Overview of ORs in final multivariate logistic regression model for each type of victimisation	71

The Victim-Offender Overlap in Prisons and Associated Challenges for Prison Managers

Table 1	Explanations for the victim-offender overlap in prisons	92

Methodological Challenges in Victimisation Studies

Table 1	Overview of advantages and disadvantages of using behavioural and general questions	146
Table 2	Examples of probes and interventions during think aloud	152
Table 3	Overview of retrieved questionnaires and response level in a Flemish study on prisoner-on-prisoner victimisation (Goossens & Daems, this volume)	162

Why Should We Study Prisoner Victimisation?

Tom Daems and Elien Goossens

1 Introduction

People in prison are usually (and often exclusively) seen and approached as persons who have committed one or more crimes and who have to pay their debt to society. However, while in prison, they often get victimised themselves. Research has demonstrated that prisons tend to be unsafe environments where various forms of victimisation take place. These forms of victimisation often go unnoticed and usually do not attract much interest from policymakers or society at large: prisoners are, indeed, far from "ideal victims" (Christie, 1986; Kury & Smartt, 2002; Lahm, 2009). However, like all human beings, also prisoners have the right to be protected from violence. The standards of the European Committee for the Prevention of Torture and Inhuman or Degrading

T. Daems (✉) · E. Goossens
Leuven Institute of Criminology (LINC), KU Leuven, Leuven, Belgium
e-mail: tom.daems@kuleuven.be

E. Goossens
e-mail: elien.goossens@kuleuven.be

Treatment or Punishment (CPT) stipulate that every member state of the Council of Europe has the obligation to provide a safe environment for those confined to prison (CPT, 2015). The European Court of Human Rights considers it a state's responsibility to secure the physical and psychological integrity of persons held in penal institutions. Indeed, prison authorities can be held accountable when a prisoner is tortured or abused because of a failure to meet the obligation to detain prisoners in a safe environment.

In recent years academic as well as policy interest in this topic has been growing, in particular in the US. The first US studies on prisoner victimisation were already conducted in the early 1960s (Bowker, 1980; Copes et al., 2011; Kury & Smartt, 2002) and this has continued well into the twenty-first century (e.g. Daquin & Daigle, 2021; Daquin et al., 2016; Grosholz & Semenza, 2021; Lahm, 2016; Rufino et al., 2012, 2013; Steiner & Wooldredge, 2020; Wolff & Shi, 2009a, 2011; Wooldredge & Steiner, 2012, 2013). This has also impacted on US criminal justice policy, such as the introduction, in 2003, of a Prison Rape Elimination Act in order to detect, stop and prevent the problem of sexual assault within the federal American prison system (Gonsalves et al., 2012; Listwan et al., 2010; Wolff et al., 2007).

Findings from American studies and US policy developments are also important for a non-US audience but at the same time we have to be careful not to generalise uncritically to other contexts, like Europe. The US prison system faces problems and challenges (in particular with respect to gang violence or mass imprisonment) which are not or to a lesser extent present in a European context (Drenkhahn & Morgenstern, 2016). Moreover, US prisoners often have less developed rights and enjoy less privacy than European prisoners whose detention conditions are monitored by the European Committee for the Prevention of Torture and Inhuman or Degrading Treatment or Punishment and the European Court of Human Rights (van Zyl Smit & Snacken, 2009). For these (and, undoubtedly, many other) reasons it is imperative that research and scholarly debate on victimisation in prisons can also take place, and flourish, in other parts of the world. In this volume we therefore focus on recent empirical work in a number of European countries (Belgium, England and Wales and The Netherlands). These chapters will be complemented with a series of reflections from a conceptual, methodological and human rights perspective.

2   Scope of the Book

Before we introduce the chapters it is useful to offer a few reflections on the scope of this book. This volume focuses on victimisation by incarcerated persons on fellow incarcerated persons. The decision to solely examine inter-prisoner victimisation was partly made on pragmatic grounds (the studies that were presented at the Leuven workshop, and that were subsequently included in this volume, all dealt with prisoner-on-prisoner victimisation) and partly on methodological grounds. Indeed, we noticed that many previous studies had failed to make a distinction based on the identity of the perpetrator. Without such a differentiation, however, incidents of victimisation committed by incarcerated persons are assumed to be similar in frequency and risk factors to those involving correctional staff. It is, however, reasonable to believe that these two forms of victimisation within prison settings are different from each other in certain aspects (Caravaca-Sánchez & Wolff, 2016; Wolff et al., 2006), and thus that researchers should consider them as separate constructs for study.

However, limiting the scope of this volume to prisoner-on-prisoner victimisation does not mean that staff-inflicted victimisation is absent, less prevalent or less significant. Indeed, abuse by prison staff can take many forms, including emotional (e.g. humiliation, verbal aggression, negative attitudes and dismissal of prisoners' concerns), physical, sexual and property-directed victimisation. It can result from both active intentional acts and passive neglectful behaviour (Bomse, 2000). Studies have described aggression in the form of being beaten out of hostility, frustration and repeated retaliation (Goldsmith et al., 2016; Rembert & Henderson, 2014; Wolff & Shi, 2009b) or excessive use of legitimate containment and control techniques (e.g. strip searches) in the face of a perceived threat (Goldsmith et al., 2016; Symkovich, 2019). In addition, staff may be guilty of "turning a blind eye", whereby they allow or even facilitate violence between prisoners (Goldsmith et al.,

2016). Refusing medical care and falling short of providing protection can also be considered forms of indirect violence committed by personnel (Bomse, 2000; Novisky et al., 2022). Moreover, the violence may be perpetrated by various individuals employed in the institution, such as supervisory staff (e.g. correctional officers and their supervisors), medical staff, those responsible for education and programme services and external employees assisting to maintain or re-establish order within prisons (e.g. anti-riot forces or police forces who intervene during a prison staff strike) (Goldsmith et al., 2016; Novisky et al., 2022; Symkovych, 2019; Wolff & Shi, 2009b).

Previous studies have found that incarcerated persons are twice as likely to report being beaten by staff (8.9%) than by fellow incarcerated persons (4.5%) (Wolff & Shi, 2009b). However, conceptual disagreement across studies and the dark number resulting from a reluctance of victims to report, or the unwillingness of some institutions to collect or disclose their recorded data, pose a challenge for researchers to arrive at reliable prevalence statistics of staff-on-prisoners violence (Goldsmith et al., 2016). Although scarce in comparison to research on prisoner-on-prisoner or prisoner-on-staff victimisation, studies on risk factors have revealed that an incarcerated person's race (e.g. Black/Hispanic individuals are at a greater risk compared to their White counterparts in US jails), the presence of mental illness, being male (for physical violence) and exhibiting certain behaviours (e.g. resistance against restraint techniques such as handcuffs and pinion restraints) are, among other variables, associated with increased risk of exposure to violence committed by staff (McNeeley, 2023; Novisky et al., 2022; Pérez et al., 2010; Semenza et al., 2023; Wolff & Shi, 2009b). Concerning staff, variables such as younger age, low job satisfaction, perceived rule violations and misconduct by co-workers, negatively perceived supervisor support, low perceptions of distributive fairness within the workplace (e.g. perceptions of fair promotions, recognition and performance ratings) and occupational-cultural drivers (e.g. "us versus them" attitudes) are, among other variables, linked to mistreatment or attitudes supportive of mistreatment and misconduct (Boateng & Hsieh, 2019; Goldsmith et al., 2016; Worley et al., 2021). These findings indicate that, in addition to the characteristics of the persons involved in violence, also working conditions and culture matter in the explanation of staff violence against incarcerated individuals. Consequently, it must be concluded that additional research into staff-inflicted victimisation is necessary and of high importance, as it will undoubtedly result in different theory models and policy recommendations.

Finally, the chapters in this book do not focus on the consequences of victimisation. From previous research we know that the consequences of victimisation perpetrated by either staff or incarcerated individuals range from physical to psychological harm and material losses. It is associated with increased feelings of unsafety during imprisonment, mental health issues, violent behaviour among incarcerated individuals and recidivism (e.g. Daquin et al., 2016; McGrath et al., 2012; Wolff & Shi, 2009b, 2011; Zweig et al., 2015). The reduction and prevention of victimisation in prisons should therefore be a priority for policymakers and prison administrations.

3   Overview of Chapters

This book includes seven chapters. In the next chapter, Jo Wilkinson examines a type of sexual assault that has been largely overlooked by past researchers, that is, incidents related to drug searches between incarcerated individuals in England and Wales. This exploration incorporates essentialist theories and social constructionist typologies. The synthesis of these perspectives leads Wilkinson to the conclusion that previous researchers have exhibited a narrow focus primarily on rape, overlooking other forms of sexual assault, particularly those arising in the context of contraband searches. She discusses her own empirical study in which a **ten-year reporting** period of administrative data was analysed to identify the individual victim and perpetrator characteristics associated with sexual victimisation and aggression. Drawing on both literature and empirical data, the chapter directs attention to the over-representation of new prisoners, young men and sex offenders as victims and perpetrators, as well as the under-representation of black and ethnically minoritised men as victims within contraband-related sexual assaults and sexual assaults overall.

In chapter "Mapping and Explaining Victimisation Among Prisoners in Flanders", Elien Goossens and Tom Daems broaden the scope to study various types of victimisation (i.e. emotional, material, physical and sexual) in Flanders, Belgium. They outline the application of general crime theories, such as opportunity and lifestyle theories, to explain victimisation behind bars. Following this, their large-scale study on prisoners' self-reported victimisation is introduced. Prevalence rates of different types of victimisation are revealed, highlighting the high frequency of emotional violence as opposed to physical or sexual incidents within Flemish prisons. Findings provide insights into the different risk factors for each type of victimisation, as well as how those risk factors can be theoretically understood based on the concepts derived from general crime theories. As observed in chapter "Who's Who? Individual Characteristics of Those Involved in Sexual Assaults in Adult Men's Prisons in England and Wales", individual characteristics contribute significantly to the understanding of victimisation in prisons. This is complemented by factors related to incarcerated persons' lifestyles (e.g. programme participation) and environmental influences that impact on the level of asserted guardianship or control (e.g. living in a shared cell). An important finding is the presence of the victim-offender overlap, a phenomenon also known in analyses of crime in free society.

The victim-offender overlap is further addressed by Esther van Ginneken in chapter "The Victim-Offender Overlap in Prisons and Associated Challenges for Prison Managers". The author argues that traditional importation and deprivation models of behaviour and adaptation of incarcerated individuals fall short in explaining victimisation and misconduct, and that they need to be complemented with insights on situational and contextual dynamics. Specifically, van Ginneken discusses the perspectives from general crime theories and the influence of drug culture in prison, as mentioned in the previous chapters. Subsequently, she adds a managerial perspective to better understand the victim-offender overlap, with a specific focus on victimisation and offending in the context of the illicit prison economy. Three challenges for prison managers are being addressed based on qualitative interview data: (1) prison managers are required to sanction addiction-driven drug use; (2) prison managers often sanction people who act under duress; and

(3) the leaders 'in charge' of the illicit economy are difficult to sanction. It is argued that safety in prisons goes beyond simply sanctioning misconduct.

While chapters "Who's Who? Individual Characteristics of Those Involved in Sexual Assaults in Adult Men's Prisons in England and Wales" till "The Victim-Offender Overlap in Prisons and Associated Challenges for Prison Managers" provide an overview of recent empirical studies on incarcerated persons' victimisation in Europe, the final three chapters reflect on conceptual, methodological and human rights considerations in the study of victimisation in prisons. In chapter "Vulnerability and Victimhood in Prison: Reflecting on the Concept of Vulnerability in Prisoner Victimisation Research", Aurore Vanliefde offers a critical reflection on processes of labelling and categorising incarcerated individuals. Vanliefde argues that within penological literature and human rights (soft) law, individuals are frequently classified as vulnerable according to personal characteristics. In this chapter, the author questions the role of this vulnerability concept in safeguarding or jeopardising individuals within correctional settings. The argument presented is that labelling individuals as vulnerable based on inherent traits can, in certain instances, be stigmatising and can be instrumentalised to reinforce power dynamics. The chapter provides food for thought on how to approach the interpretation of findings from risk factor studies, which are also covered in this book, and the formulation of policy recommendations based on these studies.

In chapter "Methodological Challenges in Victimisation Studies", Elien Goossens reflects on the methodology of self-report victimisation studies conducted within prison settings. Goossens argues that studies often fall short in terms of standardisation of measurement methods and methodological transparency. She draws on findings from studies on psychological and cognitive processes to discuss and address common threats within prison victimisation studies, including conceptualisation and operationalisation, questionnaire design, data collection and (non)response challenges. This chapter also presents recommendations aimed at enhancing the future standardisation of prison victimisation studies.

In the final chapter of this volume Tom Daems discusses the broader human rights framework in Europe with respect to preventing and responding to inter-prisoner violence and explores what role prison monitoring bodies can play to further our understanding of victimisation in prisons. Indeed, as he argues, such bodies are in a unique position to observe patterns of violence in Europe's prisons: the facilities granted to such monitoring bodies (unrestricted access to places of detention, access to documentary evidence and registers and the possibility to speak in private to prisoners and staff), enable them to get insight in prisoner victimisation which can complement the findings from victim surveys or qualitative, ethnographic research.

References

Boateng, F. D., & Hsieh, M.-L. (2019). Misconduct within the "four walls": Does organizational justice matter in explaining prison officers' misconduct and job stress? *International Journal of Offender Therapy and Comparative Criminology, 63*(2), 289–308. https://doi.org/10.1177/0306624X18780941

Bomse, A. J. (2000). Prison abuse: Prisoner-staff relations. *Guild Practitioner, 57*(4), 216–240.

Bowker, L. H. (1980). *Prison victimization*. Elsevier North-Holland.

Caravaca-Sánchez, F., & Wolff, N. (2016). Self-report rates of physical and sexual violence among Spanish inmates by mental illness and gender. *The Journal of Forensic Psychiatry & Psychology, 27*(3), 443–458. https://doi.org/10.1080/14789949.2016.1145721

Christie, N. (1986). The ideal victim. In E. Fattah (Ed.), *Crime policy to victim policy*. Macmillan.

Copes, H., Higgins, G. E., Tewksbury, R., & Dabney, D. A. (2011). Participation in the prison economy and likelihood of physical victimization. *Victims & Offenders, 6*(1), 1–18. https://doi.org/10.1080/15564886.2011.534005

CPT. (2015). *CPT standards*. Substantive sections of the CPT's general reports.

Daquin, J. C., & Daigle, L. E. (2021). The victim–offender overlap in prison: Examining the factors associated with group membership. *Journal of Interpersonal Violence, 36*(23–24), NP13439–NP13462. https://doi.org/10.1177/0886260519898427

Daquin, J. C., Daigle, L. E., & Listwan, S. J. (2016). Vicarious victimization in prison: Examining the effects of witnessing victimization while incarcerated on offender reentry. *Criminal Justice and Behavior, 43*(8), 1018–1033. https://doi.org/10.1177/0093854816650479

Drenkhahn, K., & Morgenstern, C. (2016). A European perspective on inmates' perceptions of safety. In C. Reeves (Ed.), *Experiencing imprisonment: Research on the experience of living and working in carceral institutions* (pp. 137–155). Routledge.

Goldsmith, A., Halsey, M., & Groves, A. (2016). Assaults, use of force and control. In A. Goldsmith, M. Halsey, & A. Groves (Eds.), *Tackling correctional corruption, crime prevention and security management* (pp. 83–100). Palgrave Macmillan. https://doi.org/10.1057/978-1-137-49007-0

Gonsalves, V. M., Walsh, K., & Scalora, M. J. (2012). Staff perceptions of risk for prison rape perpetration and victimization. *The Prison Journal, 92*(2), 253–273. https://doi.org/10.1177/0032885512439014

Grosholz, J. M., & Semenza, D. C. (2021). Health conditions and victimization among incarcerated individuals in U.S. jails. *Journal of Criminal Justice, 74*, 101797. https://doi.org/10.1016/j.jcrimjus.2021.101797

Kury, H., & Smartt, U. (2002). Prisoner-on-prisoner violence: Victimization of young offenders in prison. Some German Findings. *Criminal Justice, 2*(4), 411–437. https://doi.org/10.1177/17488958020020040301

Lahm, K. F. (2009). Physical and property victimization behind bars: A multilevel examination. *International Journal of Offender Therapy and Comparative Criminology, 53*(3), 348–365. https://doi.org/10.1177/0306624X08316504

Lahm, K. F. (2016). Official incidents of inmate-on-inmate misconduct at a women's prison: Using importation and deprivation theories to compare perpetrators to victims. *Criminal Justice Studies, 29*(3), 214–231. https://doi.org/10.1080/1478601X.2016.1154263

Listwan, S. J., Colvin, M., Hanley, D., & Flannery, D. (2010). Victimization, social support, and psychological well-being: A study of recently released prisoners. *Criminal Justice and Behavior, 37*(10), 1140–1159. https://doi.org/10.1177/0093854810376338

McGrath, S. A., Marcum, C. D., & Copes, H. (2012). The effects of experienced, vicarious, and anticipated strain on violence and drug use among inmates. *American Journal of Criminal Justice, 37*(1), 60–75. https://doi.org/10.1007/s12103-011-9127-1

McNeeley, S. (2023). Racial disparities in use of force against incarcerated people. *Corrections: Policy, Practice and Research, 8*(5), 406–427. https://doi.org/10.1080/23774657.2021.1900757

Novisky, M. A., Narvey, C. S., & Piquero, A. R. (2022). The keepers: Returning citizens' experiences with prison staff misconduct. *Criminal Justice and Behavior, 49*(7), 1010–1030. https://doi.org/10.1177/00938548211028895

Pérez, D. M., Gover, A. R., Tennyson, K. M., & Santos, S. D. (2010). Individual and institutional characteristics related to inmate victimization. *International Journal of Offender Therapy and Comparative Criminology, 54*(3), 378–394. https://doi.org/10.1177/0306624X09335244

Rembert, D. A., & Henderson, H. (2014). Correctional officer excessive use of force: Civil liability under section 1983. *The Prison Journal, 94*(2), 198–219. https://doi.org/10.1177/0032885514524731

Rufino, K. A., Fox, K. A., Cramer, R. J., & Kercher, G. A. (2013). The gang-victimization link: Considering the effects of ethnicity and protective behaviors among prison inmates. *Deviant Behavior, 34*(1), 25–37. https://doi.org/10.1080/01639625.2012.67989

Rufino, K. A., Fox, K. A., & Kercher, G. A. (2012). Gang membership and crime victimization among prison inmates. *American Journal of Criminal Justice, 37*(3), 321–337. https://doi.org/10.1007/s12103-011-9134-2

Semenza, D. C., Grosholz, J. M., Isom, D. A., & Novisky, M. A. (2023). Mental illness and racial disparities in correctional staff-involved violence: An analysis of jails in the United States. *Journal of Interpersonal Violence, 38*(3–4), 4138–4165. https://doi.org/10.1177/08862605221113023

Steiner, B., & Wooldredge, J. (2020). *Understanding and reducing prison violence: An integrated social control-opportunity perspective*. Routledge.

Symkovych, A. (2019). The legal and illegal use of force by prison officers in Ukraine. *The Prison Journal, 99*(1), 89–111. https://doi.org/10.1177/0032885518814728

Van Zyl Smit, D., & Snacken, S. (2009). *Principles of European prison law and policy*. Oxford University Press.

Wolff, N., Blitz, C. L., & Shi, J. (2007). Rates of sexual victimization in prison for inmates with and without mental disorders. *Psychiatric Services, 58*(8), 1087–1094. https://doi.org/10.1176/ps.2007.58.8.1087

Wolff, N., Blitz, C. L., Shi, J., Bachman, R., & Siegel, J. A. (2006). Sexual violence inside prisons: Rates of victimization. *Journal of Urban Health, 83*(5), 835–848. https://doi.org/10.1007/s11524-006-9065-2

Wolff, N., & Shi, J. (2009a). Feelings of safety inside prison among male inmates with different victimization experiences. *Violence and Victims, 24*(6), 800–816. https://doi.org/10.1891/0886-6708.24.6.800

Wolff, N., & Shi, J. (2009b). Type, source, and patterns of physical victimization a comparison of male and female inmates. *Prison Journal, 89*(2), 172–191. https://doi.org/10.1177/0032885509334754

Wolff, N., & Shi, J. (2011). Patterns of victimization and feelings of safety inside prison: The experience of male and female inmates. *Crime and Delinquency, 57*(1), 29–55. https://doi.org/10.1177/0011128708321370

Wooldredge, J., & Steiner, B. (2012). Race group differences in prison victimization experiences. *Journal of Criminal Justice, 40*(5), 358–369. https://doi.org/10.1016/j.jcrimjus.2012.06.011

Wooldredge, J., & Steiner, B. (2013). Violent victimization among state prison inmates. *Violence and Victims, 28*(3), 531–551. https://doi.org/10.1891/0886-6708.11-00141

Worley, R. M., Worley, V. B., & Lambert, E. G. (2021). Deepening the guard-inmate divide: An exploratory analysis of the relationship between staff-inmate boundary violations and officer attitudes regarding the mistreatment of prisoners. *Deviant Behavior, 42*(4), 503–517. https://doi.org/10.1080/01639625.2019.1695470

Zweig, J. M., Yahner, J., Visher, C. A., & Lattimore, P. K. (2015). Using general strain theory to explore the effects of prison victimization experiences on later offending and substance use. *The Prison Journal, 95*(1), 84–113. https://doi.org/10.1177/0032885514563283

Who's Who? Individual Characteristics of Those Involved in Sexual Assaults in Adult Men's Prisons in England and Wales

Jo Wilkinson

1 Introduction

The reporting, recording and initial response to sexual assaults in prisons in England and Wales have been an inaccessible topic for academic research. In the UK there have been various programmes to strengthen the criminal justice responses to rape and sexual assaults committed in the community, but this interest has not extended to prisons. Much of the literature about sexual victimisation in prisons is derived from studies from the United States which focus on prevalence, in anticipation of, or in response to, the US legislative intervention of the Prison Rape Elimination Act (PREA) in 2003 (Gaes & Goldberg, 2004; Nacci & Kane, 1984; Wolff et al., 2007). Other US research on victimisation in prisons has concentrated on sexual roles—consensual and

---

J. Wilkinson (✉)
University of Southampton, Southampton, UK
e-mail: jo.wilkinson@college.police.uk

College of Policing, Coventry, UK

coercive—adopted by prisoners (Bowker, 1980; Donaldson, 2001; Lockwood, 1980). The US researchers have also focused on prison officer perceptions of sexual behaviour, homosexuality, risk and sexual victimisation (Eigenberg, 2000a, 2000b; Hensley & Tewksbury, 2005; Moster & Jeglic, 2009). While there is a wealth of US research-based information on prevalence and observational studies of sexual behaviour in men's prisons, research from the United Kingdom (UK) remains sparse. Prior to the publication of this research (Wilkinson & Fleming, 2021, 2023), insights have been limited to small-scale studies which are often reliant on self-reporting by ex-prisoners (Banbury, 2004; Banbury et al., 2016; O'Donnell, 2004; Stevens, 2015, 2017). This chapter examines the published literature on the individual characteristics of those involved in prison-based sexual assaults. It provides– analysis of a ten-year period (2004–2014) of the Incident Reporting System (IRS) data derived from Her Majesty's Prison and Probation Service (formerly the National Offender Management Service). This data is based on the information recorded by prison staff in prisons in England and Wales when a sexual assault has been reported. Analysis combines a mixed-method approach to develop descriptive statistics and new information about the nature of the reported sexual assaults by coding incident descriptions which are written by prison staff in all prisons in England and Wales. The chapter provides insights into the individual-level victim and perpetrator data (rather than incident level) of those involved in sexual assaults, in terms of their time spent at the prison, criminal background, ethnicity and age.

Victimisation in prisons in England and Wales forms part of regular statistical reports published by the Ministry of Justice which are known collectively as Safety in Custody bulletins. These national statistics cover deaths in custody, self-harm and assaults. National Statistics status, as defined by the government, requires that official statistics meet the highest standards of trustworthiness, quality and public value. Sexual offences are reported under the umbrella term of 'serious assaults'. The most recent statistical bulletin (Ministry of Justice, 2023) indicated that sexual assaults in prisons are rising, along with other types of assault, following a general decrease in reporting during the COVID-19 pandemic. The pandemic-related reductions in reported assaults can be explained by the physical restrictions placed on prisoner-on-prisoner contact during that period (Ministry of Justice, 2023: 13). Serious prisoner-on-prisoner assaults increased by 28% to 1,745, in the 12 months to December 2022. The rate of prisoner-on-prisoner assaults increased 9% in the 12 months to December 2022. However, increases should be seen in the context of reduced assaults during the pandemic and incidence rates per 1,000 prisoners may provide a more accurate summary of trends. In 2022 the rate of sexual assault[1] incidents per 1,000 prisoners increased 44%, from 2.9 in 2021 to 4.2 in 2022. Data has shown—aside from the periods covered by the pandemic—a steady rise in prisoner-on-prisoner sexual assaults. For male prisoners in England and Wales, there was a 45% increase, from 215 in 2021 to 311 in 2022, with the rate increasing 40% from 2.9 to 4.0 (MoJ, 2023).

This chapter is concerned with reported adult male, prisoner-on-prisoner sexual assaults in England and Wales. The focus on male prisoners reflects Sloan's (2016: 8; 2018: 123) argument that, although men make up most of the prison population, their experience of imprisonment is normalised. She (Sloan, 2018: 123) argued that male prisoners are 'seen (while simultaneously going unseen) as the norm, the stereotype and the population that prison was designed for in the first place'. The research underpinning this article is based on analysis of the reporting data as logged by prison staff into the Incident Reporting System (IRS). It covers a ten-year period (2004–2014) and derives reports from all of men's prisons in England and Wales.

---

[1] Sexual assaults are currently defined by His Majesty's Government as any assault in England and Wales where the victim believes it to have been of a sexual nature, and where all of the following occur—they intentionally touch another person, the touching is sexual, the victim does not consent to the touching, they do not reasonably believe the other person consents and the touching can be with any part of the body or with anything else: *Safety in Custody Statistics Bulletin, England and Wales, Deaths in Prison Custody to December 2016, Assaults and Self-Harm to September 2016* (https://assets.publishing.service.gov.uk/government/uploads/system/uploads/attachment_data/file/1153237/safety-in-custody-q4-2022.pdf).

2 Explanations of Prison Sex and Sexual Victimisation in Men's Prisons

Early criminologists and penologists developed typologies to explain the sexual and violent behaviour of prisoners, often characterising 'personas' into the 'predators' and the 'victimised' and the 'masculine' and the 'feminine'. Explanations for adaptations in sexual behaviour during imprisonment have broadly used two opposing approaches. Essentialists argue that sexuality is a static and permanent trait and therefore any changes in sexual behaviour or orientation in prison are as a result of sexual deprivation. Social constructionists suggest that sexuality is fluid and based on a spectrum much wider than 'homosexual' and 'heterosexual' and is also subject to change based on cultural contexts (Eigenberg, 1992; Gibson & Hensley, 2013; Hensley et al., 2003; Stevens, 2017). Penological essentialist theories based on deprivation theories (Clemmer, 1940; Sykes, 1958) focused on the pains of imprisonment remained dominant until Groth's (1979: 125) insight into male rape in prison. Clemmer (1940: 255) first introduced the idea that sex between male prisoners was largely a result of deprivation from 'normal' heterosexual relationships. He suggested that the phenomenon of sex in prisons presented a major risk to their stability and organisation. In Sykes' (1958: 70) study of a New Jersey prison, he argued that for heterosexual men, the pains of imprisonment and lack of sexual contact with wives and girlfriends amounted to 'castration by involuntary celibacy'. For Sykes (1958: 95), sexual orientation consisted of 'habitual homosexuals' and those for whom homosexuality was a temporary consequence of sexual frustration because they could not survive prison without committing rape or engaging in homosexual activity. Sykes' (1958: 95) terminology of 'wolves, punks and fags' described sex roles and their relative associations with masculinity and femininity in the prison environment. In contrast, Groth (1979) argued that to view men who raped other men in prison as being 'heterosexually oriented' was misleading as it did not address behaviours 'more based upon exploitation than sharing'. The possibility of rape being used as a mechanism for 'playing' masculine roles, rather than being an outlet for heterosexual sexually deprived prisoners, highlighted wider problems of masculinity in men's prisons (Bowker, 1980: 12).

The term 'hypermasculinities' was coined by Toch (1998: 173) to describe the ways in which men in prison were expected to live up to masculine 'scripts', which reinforced male behaviour and induced men to target any display of more 'feminine' behaviour to differentiate themselves from it. US research provided commentaries and descriptions of sexual aggressors in prisons. Lockwood's (1980: 114) typology was based on descriptions provided by his sample of 'targets' or victims; 'gorillas' used force and surprise to rape victims, 'players' used a combination of force and threats (often using tactics to feminise their victims) and 'propositioning' in which aggressors simply made non-violent requests. Lockwood observed that 'targets' had a strong fear, not only of being raped in prison, but of the connection between prison rape and what they perceived as the permanent loss of their masculinity. Published in the same year as Lockwood's study, Bowker (1980: 11) noted that prison rape allowed heterosexual men to engage in 'sex' without damaging their self-reported heterosexuality because it facilitated them to redefine a sexual assault as being 'heterosexual' activity because prisoners identified victims as having been 'feminised' rather than raped.

Prisoner subcultures which assigned particular status to sex roles, were described in more detail by Donaldson (2001: 119) as being a stratified system in which 'men' could maintain and validate their masculinity and heterosexuality by distinguishing themselves from more effeminate prisoners. The term 'punks', used by Sykes (1958), Wooden and Parker (1982) and Donaldson (2001) referred to the lowest status group of prisoners who had been subjected to rape in prison and therefore became targets for further sexual victimisation.

Essentialist and social constructionist typologies of prison sex and victimisation have mostly focused on rape in prison and neglected other types of sexual assault such as the occurrence and impact of prisoner-on-prisoner drug or contraband searches.[2] Banbury et al.'s (2016) study introduced the first typology (based on UK research) to include drug

---

[2] From this point on, unless specified as distinct, where reference to prisoner-on-prisoner drug searches is made, this term also includes searches for other items regarded as contraband in prisons, for example, mobile phones and sim cards.

searches as a dimension of sexual assaults. The inclusion of prisoner-on-prisoner drug searches in sexual victimisation research is essential because of the proliferation of drug use in prisons in England and Wales. Wilkinson and Fleming (2021) describe prisoner-on-prisoner drug searches as being so common that they are regarded by staff and prisoners as being 'business as usual'. Hopkins and Brunton-Smith (2014: 3) noted that prisoners reported their most frequently used drug as cannabis (followed by heroin), and that their drug usage patterns prior to imprisonment tended to be mirrored during their prison sentence. Research about drugs markets that operate in prisons in England and Wales is scarce (Crewe, 2006: 148), although evidence about levels of drug use are documented (Crewe, 2009: 382; HMIP, 2014, 2015; Hopkins & Brunton-Smith, 2014). The impact of drug culture and markets on sexual assaults has been made by several studies in prisons in England and Wales (Banbury, 2004; Green et al., 2003: 255) with prisoners reporting coercive sexual activity. Coerced sexual activity may take place as 'payment' in exchange for drugs, money, phone-cards and tobacco or may be as a result of smuggling or being suspected as a smuggler. Sexual victimisation has the potential to highlight a prisoner as being involved in other exploitative relationships between prisoners, such as sexual coercion in exchange for goods and services, either as blackmail or by prisoner-on-prisoner forced drug searches (Banbury, 2004; Garland & Wilson, 2013). However, Banbury's 2004 study does not reflect the current prison drug markets associated with the use of synthetic drugs such as spice and mamba which have been identified as being the most serious threat to prisoners in recent years (HMIP, 2015; Ralphs et al., 2017). Escalation of use of synthetic cannabis has been reported to have far greater consumption rates in prisons than in the community and is associated with a decline in the use of opiates and cannabis by prisoners (Ralphs et al., 2017: 60). Research on the supply (and use) of synthetic drugs in prison drug markets is in its infancy. Acknowledgement of traditional smuggling routes such as via post, visits, staff and the extended risk associated with new and recalled prisoners have all been identified as issues regarding the general importation of drugs (Crewe, 2006: 357; 2009: 370; Wilkinson & Fleming, 2021).

Research about institutional factors linked to sexual victimisation is scarce. Some US research studies, have suggested that higher security prisons record higher incidence of sexual victimisation (Cooley, 1993; Hensley et al., 2003). Other research has suggested that higher incidence of sexual victimisation is linked to prison overcrowding, population turnover, living arrangements and the type and culture of prisons (Bowker, 1980; Fleisher & Krienert, 2006; Lockwood, 1980; Nacci & Kane, 1984; Struckman-Johnson & Struckman-Johnson, 2000; Worrall & Morris, 2011). Rather than institutional characteristics associated with sexual victimisation, the focus of this chapter is the individual characteristics associated with prisoners likely to be targeted as victims or involved in the capacity as perpetrators.

3 Methods

The analysis of sexual assaults reported in adult men's prisons in England and Wales was based on the recording data from the prisons from the Incident Reporting System (IRS). The IRS is an administrative database which was introduced in the 1980s by His Majesty's Prison and Probation Service (formerly the National Offender Management Service) to manage the recording and management of information relating to deaths in custody, self-harm and assaults. Sexual assaults are recorded as a subset of serious assaults and the recording system makes no distinction between the type of sexual assault. The IRS provides some of the source data for the official statistics which are published by the Ministry of Justice as Safety in Custody Bulletins but much of the data is not of sufficient quality to be classified as National Statistics. This is partly because data is recorded from individual prisons and is subject to variation in practices.

Following a detailed ethics process, the data was received from the National Offender Management service in 2014. It covered a full ten-year sample of adult male prisoner-on-prisoner reported sexual assault incidents in England and Wales between 2004/2005 and 2013/2014. The data was prepared as two datasets. The first of which focused on the characteristics of reported sexual assaults, including institutional and individual characteristics associated with reported sexual assaults. This dataset (referred to from here as Dataset 1) was used to produce descriptive statistical analysis of 'incidents' to identify patterns and trends. Analysis includes the type of prison, the length of time spent in the prison since reception (of the perpetrator and victim) prior to the sexual assault report, the status and category of those involved, their criminal backgrounds, age and ethnicity.

The second dataset (referred to from here as Dataset 2) was developed to identify new information derived from coding the single qualitative data field in which prison staff describe the incident and the initial response to the sexual assault. Adopting a pragmatic approach and using NVivo 10.0 software, the 844 incident descriptions were coded, and themes were identified. Coding the descriptions identified new information as it facilitated the quantification of the qualitative field. In descriptions which included sufficient information it was possible to identify, more precisely, the type of sexual assault. This was possible for 583 of the total 844 cases. Initial coding revealed information about the incident which was not available from other data fields in the IRS. For example, the type and location of the assault and mechanism used to carry it out, all of which had been identified by a number of empirical studies as an important dimension of incidents (Hensley et al., 2005; Struckman-Johnson et al., 1996; Struckman-Johnson & Struckman-Johnson, 2000).

3.1 Sample

The sample consisted of all reported adult male prisoner-on-prisoner sexual assaults in prisons in England and Wales during the data capture period of 2004/2005–2013/2014. 844 incidents of adult male prisoner-on-prisoner sexual assaults were analysed, all of which were recorded in prisons and youth offending institutions (YOIs) in England and Wales. Incidents related to sexual assaults involving staff (as victims or perpetrators), any prisoner who was under 18 at the time of the assault, all records linked to women prisoners and those mis-recorded as sexual assault were removed from the sample. The sample contained all incidents which were classified by prison staff as being a 'sexual assault' and were recorded on the IRS and managed during the data sample period by NOMS. Described in the IRS collectively as 'involvements', the 844 incidents comprised a total of 2032 prisoners, of whom 1116 were recorded as perpetrators, 826 as victims and 90 as 'other', that is, present during the reported incident, noted as a witness or with an undetermined role in the reported incident. The quality of the IRS data was poor. It was incomplete and disorganised and was transferred in separate datasets for those involved in incidents (involvements) and the incident itself, making analysis a painstaking process.

4 Individual Characteristics Associated with Prisoner-on-Prisoner Sexual Assault

This section examines the literature in respect of individual characteristics associated with both being victimised and perpetrating sexual assaults, including time since reception at the prison, criminal offence background, ethnicity and age. It examines the analysed data from the IRS and contextualises it with the relevant literature. Results are combined from Datasets 1 and 2.

The IRS data presented is dependent on incidents being identified, reported, classified and recorded by staff. It should therefore be assumed that the descriptive statistics may be incomplete and will not represent the full extent of prisoner-on-prisoner sexual assaults, which took place in men's prisons during the data period. Sexual assaults in prisons can be assumed to be under-reported (Banbury, 2004; Stevens, 2014). Decisions on what to record and how to classify a sexual assault are likely to have varied by individual officer, manager and prison, as well as being subject to variation over time. Although the IRS has the capacity to update information over time to reflect staff responses to reports of sexual assaults (including prisons and police activities), Dataset 1 did not include any signifiers to show updates and so this detail is not included.

Table 1 Type of sexual assault by role/involvement

Type of sexual assault	Victim	Perpetrator	Other	Total
Sexual assaults (other than drug searches)	441	502	52	995
Drug search	138	320	15	473
Unspecified	247	294	23	564
Total	826	1116	90	2032

Data was analysed at individual or 'involvement' level rather than incident level. Table 1 summarises the type of sexual assault by the role in the assault, or 'involvement'. Of the 583 incidents, which included enough information to determine the nature of the sexual assault, just under a quarter could be identified as being related to a prisoner-on-prisoner intimate drug or contraband search. The remainder involved other sexual assaults from verbal threats and touching to rape. This is in keeping with analysis, carried out on behalf of the Ministry of Justice by Sondhi et al. (2018), which also identified that in 40% of cases, the incident descriptions lacked sufficient information to determine more precisely the type of sexual assault that had occurred.

4.1 Being New: Time Since Reception at the Prison

Reception to prison has been recognised as being a particularly vulnerable stage of imprisonment (Bowker, 1980; Cooley, 1993; Crewe, 2009; Lockwood, 1980; Morash et al., 2012; Stevens, 2014) both in terms of self-harm related risks, and being victimised. The reception process itself, which includes removal of personal possessions and searching and showering, has been identified as accentuating the prisoner's new powerlessness and lack of status while reinforcing the dominance of prison authority (Crewe, 2009; Goffman, 1961; Toch, 1992).

The targeting of new prisoners (by established prisoners) through use of verbal abuse has been identified as an established tactic for probing vulnerability to future exploitation (Edgar et al., 2003: 33). The process of settlement into a new prison was described as a 'culture shock' by Toch (1992: 193) in which new prisoners search for information and cues from previous experience to help them transition to prison life, plan and stay safe. Lockwood's (1980: 25) study of New York State prisons found that over three-quarters of sexual 'aggression' incidents took place within 16 weeks of the 'target' entering prison, suggesting that prisoner reception centres or first transfer prisons might present the highest risk of sexual assault. Nacci and Kane (1983: 35) found that 57% of men who were victimised in Pennsylvanian federal prisons had been in their current prison for less than one month when the assault occurred. Their research with prison officers identified that staff failed to recognise a prisoner's newness to the prison as being a risk factor. Bullying in a UK young offenders' establishment was also reported to occur most frequently on the day in which new trainees arrived and on days when the dormitories were not inspected by staff. The suggestion that vulnerability could be linked to the first stages of a sentence or a move to a new institution, as well as frequency of staff supervision is supported by several studies (Garland & Wilson, 2013; McGurk & McDougall, 1991: 133). It might also be the case that newer prisoners are more likely to report sexual assaults, either because of successful initiatives delivered at the induction stages or because they are less susceptible to the inmate code and fear of 'snitching' (Fowler et al., 2010: 235). The inmate code, first described by Clemmer (1940) and Sykes (1958) describes an enforced and explicit code which regulates prisoner behaviour, relationships with prison staff and fellow prisoners, including the reporting of sexual assaults. More recent US research carried out post implementation of the PREA (Smith & Dunton, 2022), suggests that prisoners in medium-level security prisons support measures to reduce risks and confirm the view that codes about snitching do not apply to rape incidents.

The majority of the sexual 'coercion' incidents reported by Banbury's (2004: 124) study, took place early on in the served sentence of the prisoner. However, her findings did not determine whether the higher rate of sexual victimisation was because new prisoners were more likely to report than their more established counterparts. This indicates that prisons might encourage reporting by focusing some of their efforts on policies and processes which provide prevention information for prisoners during the reception and induction stages of their imprisonment or following a prison move. Alternatively, high levels of victimisation and subsequent reporting of sexual assaults may be partially explained by the proliferation of new and recalled prisoners smuggling drugs into prison by 'plugging' (Crewe, 2009; Ralphs et al., 2017) and established prisoners carrying out 'screening' for drugs through prisoner-on-prisoner searches.

Roles may be established early on during a sentence. Edgar et al. (2003: 72) argued that prisoners, when establishing themselves in a prison, may use violence to avoid being identified and labelled as a potential 'victim'. Establishing a role, or a series of roles, was identified by Edgar et al. (2003) as an important component of staying safe because he argued that prisoners' roles become fixed over time. However, suggestions that prisoner roles become fixed, does not account for changes in prisoner behaviour over the duration of a prison sentence and adaptations that they may make in response to the pains of imprisonment (Crewe, 2009: 152). Methods employed by prisoners to establish their roles may provide some insight into the phenomenon of interchangeability of victims and perpetrators in prison contexts. Ireland's (1999: 175) study of bullying identified a high frequency of violent offenders who had self-reported as being both bullies and victims and who were over twice as likely to defend themselves with violence. Similarly, Lockwood (1980: 91) identified adaptations in US prisoner behaviour and described ways in which 'targets' of sexual assault received 'warnings' of future sexual victimisation and adopted different behaviours as protective factors, such as self-isolation.

4.1.1 What the Data Shows

Table 2 indicates that prisoners were most at risk of being a victim of a sexual assault in their first three months of entering a prison. Analysis of Dataset 1 showed that six out of ten victims were sexually assaulted within three months of being received into the prison. This finding is in line with US study estimations of sexual victimisation taking place in close proximity to reception (Lockwood, 1980; Nacci & Kane, 1983). UK research by Banbury (2004: 119) also reported that 52% of victims, from her sample of 200 ex-offenders, were assaulted within one month of being imprisoned. Almost half of this sample had been subject to a multiple perpetrator sexual assault. In keeping with Banbury's (2004: 114) study, Dataset 1 showed that perpetrators tended to be in prison for longer than victims at the time of the reported sexual assault; nearly half (45%) carried out the sexual assault within their first six months since reception at the prison. Risks associated with perpetrating sexual assaults early in a prison sentence were reinforced by Banbury et al.'s (2016: 374) later research in which all 43 participants admitted to committing 'sexual coercion' in the first twelve months of their sentence, the majority admitting that they had carried out multiple sexual assaults of different types.

Analysis of Dataset 1 also identified that unclassified prisoners were over-represented as victims of sexual assault. The unclassified 'involvements' identified in Dataset 1 were new to the prison and mostly received directly from local courts, post-sentencing. Category B Local prisons in England and Wales take responsibility for security classification which influences their prisoner categorisation determining the prison at which

Table 2 Time since reception in current prison at the time of the reported sexual assault (perpetrators and victims only)

Time since reception in current prison	Role in assault[a]			
	Perpetrator		Victim	
	N	% of known[a]	N	% of known[b]
<7 days	51	6	127	16
1 week to <1 month	130	15	144	18
1 month to <3 months	199	23	209	26
3 months to <6 months	157	18	139	17
6 months to <12 months	166	19	96	12
1 to <5 years	162	18	81	10
5 years or more	12	1	7	1
Total known	877	100	803	100
Not known	239	–	23	–
Total all	1116	–	826	–

[a]The role in the assault was recorded as 'other' for 90 prisoners and they have been excluded from the table
[b]Percentages were calculated based only on those individuals where the time since their reception at that prison was known

they will serve (at least the first part of) their sentence (Grimwood, 2015).

Victims reporting sexual assaults were slightly more likely to be unclassified (36%) than perpetrators (30%) and conversely, perpetrators were more likely to be already categorised as Category B prisoners (15%) than victims (9%). It is likely that proximity to reception processes at Category B Local prisons are a factor associated with higher risks of involvement (as victims and perpetrators) in sexual assaults. Unclassified prisoners, because they have recently been received at the prison, might be at a higher risk of being targeted by other prisoners because they may have fewer protective factors (such as links to other established prisoners or gang members) and/or are believed (by other prisoners) to have concealed contraband goods (such as mobile phones or drugs).

When solely examining incidents related to drug or contraband searches, thirty-eight per cent of these occurred less than a week from reception. The clear risk of being subject to a prisoner-on-prisoner drug search shortly after reception at a prison is supported by Ralphs et al.'s (2017: 62) research in an English Category B Local prison which revealed the systematic practice of prisoners on licence using recalls to 'plug' drugs into their anus for drug supply purposes. Ralphs et al.'s (2017) research was carried out in 2015, contemporary with the IRS data capture period of 2004–2014 for this research. It therefore provides useful contextual information about drug markets, smuggling and prisoner-on-prisoner drug searches. It is not possible to determine the frequency of drug searches specifically linked to licence recalls from Dataset 1, because of missing data. Only 51 prisoners were recorded as being in prison at the time of the sexual assault, for breach of a licence or a recall.

In contrast, where sexual assaults were not identified as being related to drug searches, only 11% occurred within the first week (this analysis excludes cases where the incident type was not known). Two-thirds of prisoner-on-prisoner drug searches occurred in the first month compared to 28% of non-drug search related to other sexual assaults. This analysis is based on 563 of the 826 victims where both time since reception, and type of sexual assault were known. Sondhi et al. (2018) in their analysis of the IRS incident descriptions noted that over half of sexual assaults which didn't involve penetration with a penis seemed to be motivated by the retrieval of an item which was most often drugs. Analysis of the IRS data showed that three-quarters of these assaults were carried out within cells ($n = 134$). In both prisoner-on-prisoner drug and contraband searches and non-drug searches, victims may also have been at an increased risk because of their individual characteristics. The following sections examine how the criminal offence background, ethnicity and age of victims and perpetrators impact on being associated with reported sexual assaults.

4.2　Criminal Background

Earlier US studies have referenced the criminal background of men targeted or victimised by sexual assaults. Lockwood (1980: 25) argued that of his sample, 65% of 'targets' had served previous prison sentences and were therefore not vulnerable, first time offenders with no experience of prison. Lockwood (1980) asserted that men targeted for sexual victimisation had similar experience of prison life to those who were not targeted. Nacci and Kane's (1984: 48) study supported Lockwood's findings, as the targets identified by their research often had a substantial and obvious criminal history having been placed in the same high security prisons as their aggressor counterparts. Struckman-Johnson et al. (1996: 71) suggested that 'targets' in Midwestern US prisons, who had successfully defended themselves against attempted rape or sexual assault were more likely to have committed sex offences over their lifetime, perhaps supporting the hypothesis that sex offenders may be over-represented in prison sexual assaults. Beck et al.'s (2013: 19) much larger scale US research identified that prisoners in custody for violent sexual offences reported higher rates of sexual victimisation than counterparts convicted of other offences.

In contrast to US research evidence purporting that sex offenders are over-represented as both victims and perpetrators of sexual victimisation (Beck et al., 2013; Morash et al., 2010, 2012), Banbury's (2004: 119) UK study found that nearly half of her sample of self-reported victims of sexual coercion were on remand. The remaining half were mostly serving sentences for burglary, theft, drug offences, violence, motoring offences and robbery.

When examining the backgrounds of perpetrators of sexual assaults, Morash et al. (2010: 10) found that being sexually abused as a child, having a life sentence and having adult sexual offence convictions were predictors for committing sexual assaults involving touching other men in prison. For more serious assaults, involving threatening, attempting or carrying out 'sexual penetration', Morash et al. (2010: 8) identified that a history of committing robbery as a young person, adult sexual offence convictions, longer sentences and being young were all predictors for perpetrating sexual assaults. Their (Morash et al., 2010: 11) examination of cases of substantiated misconduct in prison (equivalent to proven adjudications in England and Wales) found that prisoners with a history of aggressive acts in prison and convictions for sexual offences (rather than property, weapons and drug-related offences) were more likely to be involved in sexual assaults involving threats, attempted penetration and penetration. Sondhi et al. (2018), in their analysis of the reporting data from England and Wales, found the most common index offence for which prisoners in the sample had been convicted, was a sexual offence.

Some of the complexities of using US research to provide context for examining reporting data from England and Wales, stems from its focus on male rape and offences connected to that, such as threats and attempts to commit male rape. The US literature largely overlooks less serious assaults, such as verbal threats and touching and does not acknowledge prisoner-on-prisoner drug searches.

4.2.1 What the Data Shows

The IRS data does not include full details of the criminal history or previous periods of imprisonment of those involved in reported sexual assaults. Data relating to the length of custodial sentence, as an indicator of the seriousness of the imprisonment offence, was incomplete and could therefore not be used in the analysis of the data. The criminal offence background of those involved in sexual assaults has been based on the sentenced offence/s for which the prisoner had been imprisoned at the time of the reported sexual assault. The IRS data included a field where staff responsible for recording sexual assaults were required to describe the offence related to the current sentence/imprisonment. This data was challenging to interpret as it was based on a wide range of crime codes and descriptions, often presented in a non-uniform manner. Once cleaned and grouped as Home Office offence types (Home Office, 2019), the offence for which the prisoner was serving a sentence was examined, as summarised in Fig. 1. A limitation of the IRS data was that analysis could not identify previous offences and/or sentences or periods of imprisonment, therefore, it was not possible to establish offending histories.

One of the most significant findings of the analysis of Dataset 1 (shown in Fig. 1), is that male victims and perpetrators who were remanded or convicted for a sexual offence were over-represented in the dataset (23%) when compared to the offence profile of the general male prison population[3] (13% of male prisoners). Conversely, those

Background offence: perpetrators and victims compared to general prison population 2009*

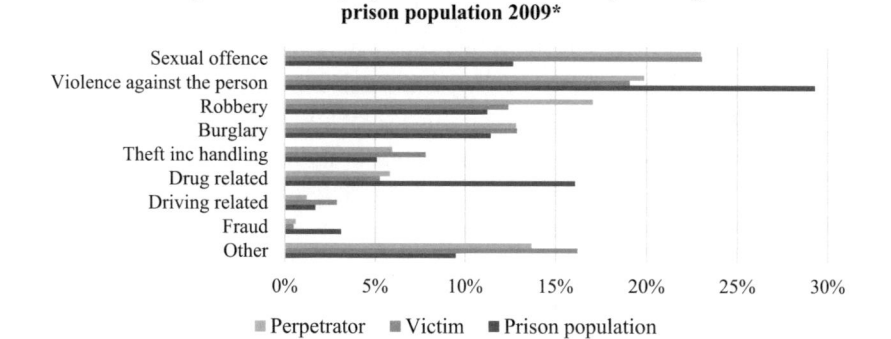

Fig. 1 Criminal offence type (grouped) of victims and perpetrators

---

[3] Where reference is made to comparisons with the general prison population, data from 2009 has been used as an example year because it is the mid-point of the data capture period. Prison population statistics were accessed from: https://www.gov.uk/government/uploads/system/uploads/attachment_data/file/218176/population-in-custody-may-2009.xls; Population in custody: monthly tables (https://assets.publishing.service.gov.uk/government/uploads/system/uploads/attachment_data/file/218175/population-in-custody-05-2009.pdf).

imprisoned for an offence of violence against the person were underrepresented (20% of those involved in sexual offence incidents compared to 29% of the male prisoner population), as were those imprisoned for drug-related offences (6% compared to 16% of the general population). The IRS data analysis indicated that perpetrators of prisoner-on-prisoner drug searches (where identifiable) were most likely to be serving a prison sentence for robbery or burglary.

Over-representation of sex offenders as perpetrators has been identified by US research (Beck et al., 2013; Miller, 2010; Morash et al., 2010: 8) suggesting that convictions for adult sex offences could be a predictor for committing sexual assault in prison. However, the over-representation of sex offenders as victims is less explicable. It is possible that because sexual offenders are usually housed separately with other sex offenders, they are more likely to be in contact with potential prison sexual assault perpetrators. Other US research (Struckman-Johnson et al., 1996: 71), suggested that sexual assault 'targets', who successfully fought off perpetrators, were also more likely to have been convicted of an adult sexual offence during their lifetime, supporting the possibility that sex offenders may target other sex offenders in prison contexts.

Banbury et al.'s (2016: 378) typology of drug search perpetrators proposed that they were likely to be drug-dependent and that most of the crimes for which they were serving sentences were acquisitive in nature such as theft, burglary and drug offences. Dataset 1 indicated that perpetrators of prisoner-on-prisoner drug searches (where known) were most likely to be serving a prison sentence for robbery or burglary. In contrast, perpetrators of other sexual assaults (where known), ranging from verbal threats to rape, were more likely to be in prison for violence against the person or sexual offences.

4.3 Ethnicity

Literature from the US has included complex, mixed explanations of the involvement of Black men as victims and perpetrators. Early US studies, such as Davis' (1968: 336) study of prison rape, suggested that there were proportionally more male Black 'aggressors' in the Philadelphia prison and that their victims were mainly White. However, Davis' (1968) early conjectures about the predominance of Black aggressors and White victims had no empirical evidence and failed to take full account of the disproportionate incarceration of Black men in Philadelphia and the US generally. A number of other pre-PREA studies reported Black men as being disproportionately involved as sexual 'aggressors' (Bowker, 1980; Carroll, 1977; Hensley et al., 2003; Lockwood, 1980; Struckman-Johnson & Struckman-Johnson, 2000). Other early pre-PREA research (Nacci & Kane, 1983, 1984) speculated that higher estimates of Black perpetrators might support their hypothesis that Black prisoners tended to congregate to commit multiple perpetrator assaults. However, although both of the Nacci and Kane (1983, 1984) papers speculated about disproportionate Black perpetrators of sexual violence, they failed to include statistics or data as supporting evidence (Gaes & Goldberg, 2004: 14). In a much later US study, Struckman-Johnson and Struckman-Johnson (2000: 386) reported a racial dimension to 'sexual coercion' in their study of Midwestern prisons where it was identified that White men were often targeted by Black men. Their data suggested that 60% of targets were White and 74% of aggressors were Black.

Post 2003, PREA US studies have continued to report mixed results about the involvement of Black men in sexual assaults in prisons. When comparing the characteristics of victims and perpetrators, Morash et al. (2012: 304), found that Black men were more likely than White men to be perpetrators and that substantiated cases identified that more than half of their matched perpetrator-victim pairs, included a Black perpetrator and a 'non-Black' victim. The same study also showed that other factors such as mass incarceration, poverty and educational background had an influence over the likelihood of becoming a perpetrator or a victim. In contrast, a number of post-PREA US studies have asserted that Black men are more likely to be sexually victimised by White perpetrators, or are as likely to be victims of sexual assaults (Jenness et al., 2007; Wolff et al., 2007) or witness them (Rowell-Cunsolo et al., 2014). Jenness et al. (2007: 42) for example, estimated that African-American prisoners in US federal prisons were more vulnerable to sexual assault than their White counterparts. Beck et al. (2013: 17) reported that rates of sexual victimisation (including men and women) were higher among White prisoners (2.9%) or prisoners of two or more ethnic backgrounds (4.0%) than incidents involving only Black prisoners (1.3%).

The US literature is difficult to apply to adult male imprisonment in England and Wales, not only because of the differences between criminal justice systems and legislation, but also because of the higher rate of incarceration and the wider significance of the disproportional imprisonment of Black, Asian and ethnic minority men in the US. In 2014, at the end of the IRS data capture period of 2004–2014, Rowell-Cunsolo et al. (2014: 55) reported that Black men were eight times more likely to be imprisoned than White men in the US and if this trend were to continue, one in three Black men should expect to be imprisoned during their lifetime.

Examining the criminal justice system in England and Wales, disproportionality in the treatment of people from minority ethnic backgrounds has been consistently identified by official data. Data from 2020, published by the Ministry of Justice (2021: 1) reported that minority ethnic groups are over-represented at many stages throughout the criminal justice system when compared with the White ethnic group and the population breakdown in England and Wales. The data indicated that the greatest disparity is apparent in police stop and searches, custodial remands and prison population. Custodial sentencing trends were also highlighted as varying between ethnic groups (MoJ, 2021) where Black prisoners served the greatest proportion of their original sentence in custody. In terms of the prison population, Black offenders made up 32% of the prison population for under-18-year olds, despite accounting for only 13% of the whole prison population. Mixed ethnic groups made up 12% of all prisoners under 18, yet only accounted for 5% of the whole prison population.

There is limited research on ethnic minority prisoner involvement in prison-based sexual assaults in England and Wales or the UK. One study of 'sexual coercion' in England and Wales (Banbury, 2004) reported that ethnic minority prisoners were infrequently reported to be involved in 'sexual coercion' but frequently reported experiencing racial abuse and harassment during prison-authorised (staff on prisoner) drug and strip searches. Prisoners in Banbury's (2004: 126) sample said that these incidents of racial abuse often went unreported to the prison authorities because the racial abuse had been perpetrated by staff. The divergence in evidence about ethnicity and risk of victimisation has been cited as a gap in the knowledge base, requiring further examination (O'Donnell, 2004; Pérez et al., 2010; Rowell-Cunsolo et al., 2014). Explanations of Black men as predominate perpetrators in the US prison system have failed to consider or measure the impact of competing factors which might marginalise them or change their reporting behaviour (Morash et al., 2012).

4.3.1 What the Data Shows

Ethnic background was identified for nearly all victims and perpetrators (98%). The ethnicity field of data was distinct as being one of the most complete and clean from the entire IRS dataset. Of those involved (as victims or perpetrators) in sexual assaults, 80% were designated as White. In contrast to the suggestion of much of the pre-PREA US literature (Bowker, 1980; Carroll, 1977; Hensley et al., 2003; Lockwood, 1980; Nacci & Kane, 1983, 1984; Struckman-Johnson & Struckman-Johnson, 2000), the proportion of individuals from Black, Asian and ethnic minority backgrounds, involved as perpetrators of sexual assaults were proportionate to their make-up of the general prison population (26% compared with approximately 25% of the general male prison population over the period). This conclusion is in keeping with Sondhi et al.'s (2018) analysis of the reporting data. However, this study identified that ethnic minority prisoners were under-represented as victims of sexual assaults (10%, $N = 83$). Under-representation as victims in the data may be explained by ethnic minority prisoners being less willing to report sexual assaults, perhaps because of lack of confidence in the criminal justice system or as a result of a stronger allegiance to the principles of the inmate code. The literature on ethnicity and reporting sexual assault is inconclusive and mostly based on US research. Garland and Wilson (2013: 1215), identified that Black prisoners were

Table 3 Ethnicity (grouped) of victims and perpetrators

Ethnicity (grouped)	Role in sexual assault							
	Perpetrator		Victim		Others (e.g. present)		Total	
	N	% of known	N	% of known	N	% of known	N	% of known
White	813	73	731	88	74	82	1618	80
BAME total	286	26	83	10	12	13	381	19
Of which: mixed race	53	5	10	1	2	2	65	3
Asian	48	4	37	4	3	3	88	4
Black	184	16	36	4	7	8	227	11
Any other	1	0	0	–	0	–	1	0
Not stated	17	2	12	1	4	4	33	2
Total	1116	100	826	100	90	100	2032	100

less likely than White counterparts to view reporting as 'snitching'. Similarly, Fowler (2010: 236) found that Black prisoners in America were the most likely ethnic group to report sexual victimisation, going as far as suggesting that interventions aimed at encouraging reporting were targeted at White prisoners. However, disparities in the way that prisoners perceive reporting are unlikely to account for the difference in its entirety (Table 3).

4.3.2 Ethnicity by Type of Sexual Assault

The data indicates that Black, Asian and ethnic minority perpetrators were over-represented in prisoner-on-prisoner drug searches. Analysis showed that 41% of perpetrators in these incidents were from ethnic minorities, when they only accounted for a quarter of the overall perpetrator population and general prison population. White prisoners were under-represented (making up 73% of the perpetrators overall but only 59% of those involved in prisoner-on-prisoner drug searches. Crewe (2006: 362) noted, from his study of an English Category C prison, that different ethnic groups held different levels of 'social power' which shaped the organisation of drug dealing. Poor data quality meant that it was not possible to accurately analyse ethnic background by role in prisoner-on-prisoner drug searches. In all other types of sexual assault, for example, verbal threats to anal rape, the ethnic background of the perpetrators was in keeping with the overall perpetrator population.

Garland and Wilson's (2013: 1215) research suggested that the extent to which prisoners experienced 'prisonisation' or acceptance of prison life and culture, impacted on rates of reporting. This may provide a useful framework for further research to ascertain the reasons for ethnic differences in reporting rates. Where prisonisation may be strengthened by increased exposure to the criminal justice system, ethnic minority groups may have stronger resolve to adhere to informal rules about 'anti-snitching' and weakened motivation to report sexual assaults. Although Garland and Wilson (2013: 1215) reported that Black men were much less likely to view reporting of sexual assaults as snitching, they speculated that gang membership, delineated by race and the informal codes related to them, might have had a strong impact on reducing reporting levels. Beck et al.'s (2013: 17) large-scale US research on the prevalence of sexual victimisation for male and female prisoners reported that rates were higher among White prisoners (2.9%) or prisoners of two or ethnic backgrounds (4.0%) than incidents involving only Black prisoners (1.3%).

4.3.3 Ethnicity by Number of Perpetrators

When looking only at those incidents where the number or perpetrators was known (722 of the 844 incidents), perpetrators from a Black, Asian or ethnic minority background were more likely to be involved than their White counterparts in incidents involving multiple perpetrators. Comparisons of involvement in multiple perpetrator incidents showed that 61% ($N = 165$) of Black, Asian or ethnic minority perpetrators ($N = 269$) were named as being involved compared to 41% ($N = 318$) of White perpetrators ($N = 779$). Black, Asian and ethnic minority victims were also slightly more likely to be involved in incidents involving multiple perpetrators (27%) than White victims (20%). The majority (75%) of sexual assaults involved prisoners from the same ethnic background.

4.4 Age, Appearance and Sexuality

Reliable evidence about the impact of age on reporting sexual assaults in prison contexts is limited (Miller, 2010: 703). In the US context, Bowker (1980: 11) argued that male victims of rape and sexual violence were more likely to be middle-class, young, inexperienced, convicted of minor property offences and slight in build. He suggested that a key to their selection as a target for sexual victimisation was other prisoners' assessment of their vulnerability to being overpowered. Wooden and Parker (1982: 99) found that heterosexual men who reported being sexually assaulted were, on average, 23 years old and younger than the average age of the prison population, which was 29 years old. The vulnerability of younger male prisoners being sexually victimised, particularly on transfer or initial reception to a prison, has been the subject of discussion in several studies (Morash et al., 2012; Pérez et al., 2010; Stevens, 2014; Tewksbury, 1989) but is not necessarily supported by reliable empirical evidence. Beck et al.'s (2013: 6) large-scale survey of US prisoners in prisons and jails between 2011 and 2012 suggested that juveniles (aged 16–17), who were housed in adult facilities, reported slightly lower rates (1.8%) of sexual victimisation than adult prisoners in prisons (2%) and jails (1.6%). In the US, 'jails' typically house people awaiting trial and serving short sentences, while 'prisons' house longer-term prisoners. Among male and female prisoners, age was not identified as a significant factor in rates of sexual victimisation in state and federal prisons, with the exception that prisoners aged 55 or older reported slightly lower rates of victimisation. In jails, fulfilling similar functions to local prisons in the UK, sexual victimisation rates were lower for prisoners in older-age categories (35 onwards) than for prisoners aged 20–24 (Beck et al., 2013: 18). This pattern of lower reporting for older-age groups may be partially explained by Miller's (2010: 703) observations that older prisoners in the

US had 'aged behind bars' and may be more strongly compliant with the inmate code.

Previous literature, mostly from the US (Bowker, 1980; Hensley et al., 2005; Morash et al., 2012; Trammell, 2011) has suggested that characteristics such as appearance (related to age and femininity), sexuality or gender presentation may influence decisions made by established prisoners to target new entrants. Additional barriers in deciding to report in a male prison context may often relate to commonly held myths about male rape (Mezey & King, 2000; Scarce, 1997; Turchik & Edwards, 2012). Structured masculinity in social institutions, including prisons, may be based on power derived from socialisation of ideas about sexuality, in which 'doing heterosexuality' validates masculinity (Jewkes, 2005: 59). The notion of 'less masculine' men being labelled in prison as 'feminine' and therefore becoming targets for sexual victimisation (Bowker, 1980; Connell, 2005; Donaldson, 2001; Lockwood, 1980) has been identified as a feature of emasculation. Bowker (1980: 11) reported that following sexual victimisation, prisoners were often referred to as 'girls' by other prisoners, which served to emasculate them and 'reclassify' the rape as 'heterosexual' rather than 'homosexual'. Eigenberg (2000a: 437) made the point that theories of gender and sexuality traditionally examined relative male and female power, and regarded rape as an expression of patriarchy.

Common assumptions that homosexual men or men who have sex with men are at higher risk of sexual victimisation in prisons are supported by much of the research (Bowker, 1980; Eigenberg, 1994; Hensley et al., 2005; Jenness et al., 2007). One of the challenges of assessing risk associated with sexuality is the fluidity by which some men describe their sexuality while in prison (Stevens, 2013, 2017) and their disinclination to self-report same-sex sexual behaviour (Taylor et al., 2013). Nacci and Kane's (1983: 35) US study identified that 28% of prisoners, from their single-prison sample, reported having had a homosexual experience but only 3% of those self-identified as being gay or bisexual. They identified that 70% of the men who had self-identified as homosexual or bisexual were categorised by other prisoners as being potential 'targets' for sexual victimisation. There is little research about gender assignment and sexual victimisation. In a study of Californian prisons, Jenness et al. (2007: 42) argued that prisoners designated as 'non-heterosexual' or 'transsexual' were more likely to become victims of sexual assault than their heterosexual counterparts. Miles-Johnson's (2013: 8) Australian research found that lesbian, gay, bisexual, transgender and intersex (LGBTI) victims of non-prison-based crime were less willing to report crime to the police than their heterosexual counterparts. The lack of UK and US research on the experience of trans prisoners, is notable.

Although masculinity and sexuality form part of the US literature on sexual victimisation in prisons, this information was not possible to derive from the IRS data as sexuality and gender presentation were not recorded as part of the IRS reporting process.

4.4.1 What the Data Shows

Younger-age groups were over-represented in the sexual assault data. Two-thirds of victims (66%) and over half of perpetrators (55%) were under 30 at the time of the assault, while only accounting for just under half of the average general prison population throughout the period. There was no identifiable difference between the proportion of prisoners aged under 30 who were victims of prisoner-on-prisoner drug searches (62%) or other sexual assaults (65%). Outcomes for perpetrators were proportionate to their age profile in the IRS dataset apart from those under 30 years of age who were less likely to have a recorded outcome of 'referred to police' (45%) than expected. Dataset 1 excluded prisoners and incidents involving any person under eighteen years of age and so analysis for this group is unavailable.

The average age at the time of the assault for both victims and perpetrators was approximately 30 years, although the age most commonly reported (the mode or most frequently occurring) was notably younger: 24 years for perpetrators ($N = 66$) and 21 for victims ($N = 71$). This finding is in keeping with the Sondhi et al. (2018) age profile of male and female victims and perpetrators. Banbury et al.'s (2016: 378) study noted that the age of drug search perpetrators varied considerably but averaged at under 33 years. The US literature on the incidence and prevalence of sexual assaults reported that being younger presented risks of sexual victimisation (Beck et al., 2013; Morash et al., 2012). However, Morash et al. (2012) and Beck et al. (2013) focused on rape and attempted rape in prisons, with no reference to less serious sexual assaults or prisoner-on-prisoner drug or contraband searches. Beck et al.'s (2013: 6) survey of US prisoners in prisons and jails between 2011 and 2012 found that juveniles (aged 16–17), housed in adult facilities, reported slightly lower rates (1.8%) of sexual victimisation than adult prisoners in prisons (2%) and jails (1.6%) but that older prisoners had lower than average rates of sexual victimisation. The same study (Beck et al., 2013: 18) reported that sexual victimisation rates, particularly in jails which are broadly comparable to local prisons in England and Wales, were lower for prisoners in older-age categories (35 onwards) than for prisoners aged 20–24, in keeping with the analysis of the IRS data).

Miller's (2010: 703) assertion that older prisoners were less likely to report sexual assaults because they had spent more time in prison and internalised the inmate code may explain patterns found from the IRS data. Several US studies have identified that the likelihood of reporting declines as time served increases (Fowler et al., 2010: 232; Garland & Wilson, 2013: 1213).

5 Conclusion

This chapter provides insights into the individual characteristics of those involved in prisoner-on-prisoner sexual assaults recorded in adult men's prisons ($N = 844$) in England and Wales. Findings are based on a ten-year reporting period (2004–2014) using data recorded on the Incident Reporting System (IRS) from His Majesty's Prison and Probation Service (formerly known as the National Offender Management Service). It has examined trends in the characteristics of adult male victims and perpetrators, including time since arrival or reception at the prison, criminal offence background, ethnicity and age. The relevance and risk of being new in a prison was reinforced by descriptive data analysis of prisoner categorisation at the time of reporting the incident. Data confirmed that unclassified prisoners were over-represented in the data as both victims and perpetrators. Category B Local prisons in England and Wales were identified as potential hotspots of risk for sexual assault, most often experienced in an individual's first three months of reception at a prison. Reception stage risks extended to perpetrators too, as almost half of them committed sexual assaults in the first six months of being at a prison. Prisoner-on-prisoner drug searches, only identifiable through analysis of the qualitative incident descriptions, were clearly associated with the early or reception stages at a prison, as 38% of these were reported as occurring less than a week from reception at a prison. Incidents involving prisoners new to a prison reinforce evidence that the reception stage represents a high risk period for most prisoners (Crewe, 2009). These incidents may include cases where new arrivals are targeted because of widely held beliefs among prisoners that new or recalled prisoners may be 'plugged' with drugs (Ralphs et al., 2017). Increased reports by new prisoners may also indicate an augmented willingness to report early on in serving a sentence (Garland & Wilson, 2013).

The criminal offence background of those involved in sexual assaults provided confirmation that prisoners serving sentences for sex offences were over-represented as both victims and perpetrators. In contrast, those imprisoned for an offence of violence against the person or for drug-related offences were under-represented when compared to the general male prison population. Analysis of perpetrators of prisoner-on-prisoner drug searches showed that they were most likely to be serving a prison sentence for robbery or burglary.

The IRS data revealed that most victims and perpetrators were designated as being White. In contrast to Morash et al.'s US study (2012: 304) which suggested that Black men were more likely than White men to be perpetrators (and victims 'non-Black'), the IRS data analysis found Black, Asian and ethnic minority perpetrators were proportionate to their make-up in the general prison population. Dataset 1 identified that Black, Asian and ethnic minority prisoners were under-represented as reported victims of sexual assault, raising questions about victimisation levels and willingness to report incidents in England and Wales. Implementation of the PREA suggests some changes in the way prisoners perceive rape, indicating that it is seen more as an issue about safety rather than snitching (Smith & Dunton, 2022: 14).

Analysis of the data also exposed that in the majority of incidents the victim was able to name the perpetrator/s, perhaps reinforcing the real problems associated with breaching the inmate code by making a report and the difficulties for staff in responding to and investigating sexual assaults. Remarkably, even though most incidents were reported directly to a member of prison staff (usually a prison officer), in almost a third of the incidents there was not enough information recorded to establish the precise nature of the sexual assault. This may be, in part, explained by the function of the IRS data as a managerial system rather than one designed for the purposes of analysis and research. The lack of accurate recording of sexual assaults in the IRS indicated that the focus was on outputs, process and audit, possibly at the expense of including information that had the potential to realise improved safety in custody (Wilkinson & Fleming, 2023). Missing data reduced the scope analysis in a number of areas, particularly where individual-level data meant that the nature of a person's involvement was unclear. The ten-year period is also likely to have included changes in recording practices between each prison and the management of the data itself. All of these issues in recording factors require caution in the interpretation of the findings.

Using administrative data limits findings to trends rather than an examination of possible causes for the reported sexual assaults in prison settings. Without wider research about the experience and attitudes of prisoners and prison staff, the meaning and motivations behind such incidents remain obscured. Statistics alone can only describe information as it has been reported and recorded. Statistics that lack context and presume incidents are reported and recorded neutrally and without intent. They cannot convey the prisoner experience, pains of victimisation and negotiation involved in deciding to report a sexual assault in a hostile environment.

References

Banbury, S. (2004). Coercive sexual behaviour in British prisons as reported by adult ex-prisoners. *The Howard Journal of Criminal Justice, 43*(2), 113–130. https://doi.org/10.1111/j.1468-2311.2004.00316.x

Banbury, S., Lusher, J., & Morgan, W. (2016). Male sexual aggressors in the British prison service: An exploratory study. *International Journal of Mental Health and Addiction, 14*(4), 370–384. https://doi.org/10.1007/s11469-016-9678-y

Beck, A. J., Berzofsky, M., Caspar, R., & Krebs, C. (2013). *Sexual victimization in prisons and jails reported by inmates, 2011–12*. Bureau of Justice Statistics. https://bjs.ojp.gov/content/pub/pdf/svpjri1112.pdf

Bowker, L. (1980). *Prison victimization*. Elsevier.

Carroll, L. (1977). Humanitarian reform and biracial sexual assault in a maximum security prison. *Journal of Contemporary Ethnography, 5*(4), 417–437. https://doi.org/10.1177/089124167700500402

Clemmer, D. (1940). *The prison community*. Holt, Rinehart & Winston.

Connell, R. (2005). *Masculinities*. University of California Press.

Cooley, D. (1993). Criminal victimization in male federal prisons. *Canadian Journal of Criminology, 35*(4), 479–495. https://doi.org/10.3138/cjcrim.35.4.479

Crewe, B. (2006). Prison drug dealing and the ethnographic lens. *Howard Journal of Crime and Justice, 45*(4), 347–368.

Crewe, B. (2009). *The prisoner society: Power, adaptation, and social life in an English prison*. Oxford University Press.

Davis, A. J. (1968). Sexual assaults in the Philadelphia prison system and Sheriff's Vans. *Trans-Action, 6*, 8–17. https://doi.org/10.1007/BF03180854

Donaldson, S. (2001). A million jockers, punks and queens. In D. Sabo, T. Kupers, & W. London (Eds.), *Prison masculinities* (pp. 118–126). Temple University Press.

Edgar, K., O'Donnell, I., & Martin, C. (2003). *Prison violence: The dynamics of conflict, fear and power*. Willan Cullompton.

Eigenberg, H. M. (1992). Homosexuality in male prisons: Demonstrating the need for a social constructionist approach. *Criminal Justice Review, 17*(2), 219–234. https://doi.org/10.1177/073401689201700204

Eigenberg, H. M. (1994). Rape in male prisons: Examining the relationship between correctional officers' attitudes toward male rape and their willingness to respond to acts of rape. In M. Braswell, R. Montgomery, & L. Lombardo (Eds.), *Prison violence in America* (pp. 145–165). Routledge.

Eigenberg, H. M. (2000a). Correctional officers and their perceptions of homosexuality, rape, and prostitution in male prisons. *The Prison Journal, 80*(4), 415–433. https://doi.org/10.1177/0032885500080004007

Eigenberg, H. M. (2000b). Correctional officers' definitions of rape in male prisons. *Journal of Criminal Justice, 28*(5), 435–449. https://doi.org/10.1016/S0047-2352(00)00057-X

Fleisher, M., & Krienert, J. (2006). *The culture of prison sexual violence.* https://www.ojp.gov/pdffiles1/nij/grants/216515.pdf

Fowler, S. (2010). Would they officially report an in-prison sexual assault? An examination of inmate perceptions. *The Prison Journal, 90*(2), 220–243.

Fowler, S. K., Blackburn, A. G., Marquart, J. W., & Mullings, J. L. (2010). Would they officially report an in-prison sexual assault? An examination of inmate perceptions. *The Prison Journal, 90*(2), 220–243. https://doi.org/10.1177/0032885510363387

Gaes, G., & Goldberg, A. (2004). *Prison rape: A critical review of the literature.* National Institute of Justice.

Garland, B., & Wilson, G. (2013). Prison inmates' views of whether reporting rape is the same as snitching: An exploratory study and research agenda. *Journal of Interpersonal Violence, 28*(6), 1201–1222. https://doi.org/10.1177/0886260512468238

Gibson, L. E., & Hensley, C. (2013). The social construction of sexuality in prison. *The Prison Journal, 93*(3), 355–370. https://doi.org/10.1177/0032885513490503

Goffman, E. (1961). *Asylums. Essays on the social situation of mental patients and other inmates.* Penguin.

Green, J., Strang, J., Hetherton, J., Whiteley, C., Heuston, J., & Maden, T. (2003). Same-sex sexual activity of male prisoners in England and Wales. *International Journal of STD & AIDS, 14*(4), 253–257. https://doi.org/10.1258/095646203321264863

Grimwood, G. (2015). *Categorisation of prisoners in the UK* (Briefing Paper Number 07437). Library, H.o.C.

Groth, A. (1979). *Men who rape: The psychology of the offender.* Plenum.

Hensley, C., Koscheski, M., & Tewksbury, R. (2005). Examining the characteristics of male sexual assault targets in a southern maximum-security prison.

Journal of Interpersonal Violence, 20(6), 667–679. https://doi.org/10.1177/0886260505276069

Hensley, C., & Tewksbury, R. (2005). Wardens' perceptions of prison sex. *The Prison Journal, 85*(2), 186–197. https://doi.org/10.1177/0032885505276996

Hensley, C., Wright, J., Tewksbury, R., & Castle, T. (2003). The evolving nature of prison argot and sexual hierarchies. *The Prison Journal, 83*(3), 289–300. https://doi.org/10.1177/0032885503256330

HMIP. (2014). *HM chief inspector of prisons for England and Wales: Annual report 2013–2014*. Her Majesty's Inspectorate of Prisons. https://www.justiceinspectorates.gov.uk/hmiprisons/wp-content/uploads/sites/4/2014/10/HMIP-AR_2013-14.pdf

HMIP. (2015). *Changing patterns of substance misuse in adult prisons and service responses: Thematic report*. Her Majesty's Inspectorate of Prisons. https://www.justiceinspectorates.gov.uk/hmiprisons/wp-content/uploads/sites/4/2015/12/Substance-misuse-web-2015.pdf

Home Office. (2019). *Offence classification index*. Home Office.

Hopkins, K., & Brunton-Smith, I. (2014). *Prisoners' experience of prison and outcomes on release: Waves 2 and 3 of SPCR: Results from the Surveying Prisoner Crime Reduction (SPCR) longitudinal cohort study of prisoners*. Ministry of Justice Analytical Series. https://assets.publishing.service.gov.uk/media/5a7d94d3e5274a676d532e9c/prisoners-experience-of-prison-and-outcomes-on-release-waves-2-and-3-spcr.pdf

Ireland, J. L. (1999). Bullying behaviors among male and female prisoners: A study of adult and young offenders. *Aggressive Behavior, 25*(3), 161–178. https://doi.org/10.1002/(SICI)1098-2337(1999)25:3%3c161::AID-AB1%3e3.0.CO;2-#

Jenness, V., Maxson, C. L., Matsuda, K. N., & Sumner, J. M. (2007). *Violence in California correctional facilities: An empirical examination of sexual assault*. Center for Evidence-Based Corrections Department of Criminology. https://bpb-us-e2.wpmucdn.com/sites.uci.edu/dist/0/1149/files/2013/06/BulletinVol2Issue2.pdf

Jewkes, Y. (2005). Men behind bars: "Doing" masculinity as an adaptation to imprisonment. *Men and Masculinities, 8*(1), 44–63. https://doi.org/10.1177/1097184X03257452

Lockwood, D. (1980). *Prison sexual violence*. Elsevier.

McGurk, B., & McDougall, C. (1991). *The prevention of bullying among incarcerated delinquents*. David Fulton Publishing Ltd.

Mezey, G., & King, M. (2000). *Male victims of sexual assault*. Oxford University Press.

Miles-Johnson, T. (2013). LGBTI variations in crime reporting: How sexual identity influences decisions to call the cops. *SAGE Open, 3*(2), 1–15. https://doi.org/10.1177/2158244013490707

Miller, K. L. (2010). The darkest figure of crime: Perceptions of reasons for male inmates to not report sexual assault. *Justice Quarterly, 27*(5), 692–712. https://doi.org/10.1080/07418820903292284

Ministry of Justice. (2021). *National statistics: Ethnicity and the criminal justice system, 2020*. https://www.gov.uk/government/statistics/ethnicity-and-the-criminal-justice-system-statistics-2020/ethnicity-and-the-criminal-justice-system-2020

Ministry of Justice. (2023). *Safety in custody statistics, England and Wales: Deaths in prison custody to March 2023 assaults and self-harm to December 2022*. https://www.gov.uk/government/statistics/safety-in-custody-quarterly-update-to-december-2022/safety-in-custody-statistics-england-and-wales-deaths-in-prison-custody-to-march-2023-assaults-and-self-harm-to-december-2022

Morash, M., Jeong, S., Bohmert, M. N., & Bush, D. R. (2012). Men's vulnerability to prisoner-on-prisoner sexual violence: A state correctional system case study. *The Prison Journal, 92*(2), 290–311. https://doi.org/10.1177/0032885512439185

Morash, M., Jeong, S. J., & Zang, N. L. (2010). An exploratory study of the characteristics of men known to commit prisoner-on-prisoner sexual violence. *The Prison Journal, 90*(2), 161–178. https://doi.org/10.1177/0032885510361826

Moster, A. N., & Jeglic, E. L. (2009). Prison warden attitudes toward prison rape and sexual assault: Findings since the Prison Rape Elimination Act (PREA). *The Prison Journal, 89*(1), 65–78. https://doi.org/10.1177/0032885508329981

Nacci, P. L., & Kane, T. R. (1983). The incidence of sex and sexual aggression in federal prisons. *Federal Probation, 47*(4), 31.

Nacci, P. L., & Kane, T. R. (1984). Sex and sexual aggression in federal prisons—Inmate involvement and employee impact. *Federal Probation, 48*(1), 46–53.

O'Donnell, I. (2004). Prison rape in context. *British Journal of Criminology, 44*(2), 241–255. https://doi.org/10.1093/bjc/44.2.241

Pérez, D. M., Gover, A. R., Tennyson, K. M., & Santos, S. D. (2010). Individual and institutional characteristics related to inmate victimization.

International Journal of Offender Therapy and Comparative Criminology, 54(3), 378–394. https://doi.org/10.1177/0306624X09335244

Ralphs, R., Williams, L., Askew, R., & Norton, A. (2017). Adding spice to the porridge: The development of a synthetic cannabinoid market in an English prison. *The International Journal of Drug Policy, 40*, 57–69. https://doi.org/10.1016/j.drugpo.2016.10.003

Rowell-Cunsolo, T. L., Harrison, R. J., & Haile, R. (2014). Exposure to prison sexual assault among incarcerated black men. *Journal of African American Studies, 18*(1), 54–62. https://doi.org/10.1007/s12111-013-9253-6

Scarce, M. (1997). *Male on male rape: The hidden toll of stigma and shame.* Basic Books.

Sloan, J. (2016). *Masculinities and the adult male prison experience.* Springer Nature.

Sloan, J. (2018). Saying the unsayable: Foregrounding men in the prison system. In M. Maycock & K. Hunt (Eds.), *New perspectives on prison masculinities* (pp. 123–144). Palgrave Macmillan.

Smith, H. P., & Dunton, C. A. (2022). The Prison Rape Elimination Act (PREA): Snitching, sexuality, and normalizing deviance. *International Journal of Offender Therapy and Comparative Criminology*, 1–18. https://doi.org/10.1177/0306624X221113530

Sondhi, J., Hinks, S., & Smith, H. (2018). *Sexual assaults reported in prisons: Exploratory findings from analysis of incident descriptions.* Ministry of Justice.

Stevens, A. (2013). *Consensual sex among men in prison.* Commission on Sex in Prison, the Howard League for Penal Reform. https://howardleague.org/wp-content/uploads/2016/03/consensual_sex_in_prison.pdf

Stevens, A. (2014). *Coercive sex in prison.* Commission on Sex in Prison, the Howard League for Penal Reform. https://howardleague.org/wp-content/uploads/2016/03/Coercive-sex-in-prison.pdf

Stevens, A. (2015). *Sex in prison: Experiences of former prisoners.* Commission on Sex in Prison, the Howard League for Penal Reform. https://howardleague.org/wp-content/uploads/2016/03/Sex-in-prison-web.pdf

Stevens, A. (2017). Sexual activity in British men's prisons: A culture of denial. *British Journal of Criminology, 57*(6), 1379–1397. https://doi.org/10.1093/bjc/azw094

Struckman-Johnson, C., & Struckman-Johnson, D. (2000). Sexual coercion rates in seven midwestern prison facilities for men. *The Prison Journal, 80*(4), 379–390.

Struckman-Johnson, C., Struckman-Johnson, D., Rucker, L., Bumby, K., & Donaldson, S. (1996). Sexual coercion reported by men and women in prison. *The Journal of Sex Research, 33*(1), 67–76. https://doi.org/10.1080/00224499609551816

Sykes, G. (1958). *The society of captives*. Princeton University Press.

Taylor, A., Munro, A., Allen, E., Dunleavy, K., Cameron, S., Miller, L., & Hickman, M. (2013). Low incidence of hepatitis C virus among prisoners in Scotland. *Addiction, 108*(7), 1296–1304. https://doi.org/10.1111/add.12107

Tewksbury, R. (1989). Fear of sexual assault in prison inmates. *The Prison Journal, 69*(1), 62–71. https://doi.org/10.1177/003288558906900109

Toch, H. (1992). *Living in prison. The ecology of survival*. USA American Psychological Society.

Toch, H. (1998). Hypermasculinities and prison violence. In L. Bowker (Ed.), *Masculinities and violence* (pp. 168–178). Sage.

Trammell, R. (2011). Symbolic violence and prison wives: Gender roles and protective pairing in men's prisons. *The Prison Journal, 91*(3), 305–324. https://doi.org/10.1177/0032885511409891

Turchik, J. A., & Edwards, K. M. (2012). Myths about male rape: A literature review. *Psychology of Men & Masculinity, 13*(2), 211–226. https://doi.org/10.1037/a0023207

Wilkinson, J., & Fleming, J. (2021). Prisoner-on-prisoner drug searches in prisons in England and Wales: 'Business as usual.' *Incarceration, 2*(2), 1–17. https://doi.org/10.1177/26326663211015852

Wilkinson, J., & Fleming, J. (2023). Practice without prospect: The imaginary response to the recording and investigations of sexual assault in prison. *Theoretical Criminology*, 1–17. https://doi.org/10.1177/13624806231184825

Wolff, N., Blitz, C. L., & Shi, J. (2007). Rates of sexual victimization in prison for inmates with and without mental disorders. *Psychiatric Services, 58*(8), 1087–1094. https://doi.org/10.1176/ps.2007.58.8.1087

Wooden, W. S., & Parker, J. (1982). *Men behind bars: Sexual exploitation in prison*. Plenum.

Worrall, J. L., & Morris, R. G. (2011). Inmate custody levels and prison rule violations. *The Prison Journal, 91*(2), 131–157. https://doi.org/10.1177/0032885511404380

Mapping and Explaining Victimisation Among Prisoners in Flanders

Elien Goossens and Tom Daems

1 Introduction

This chapter aims to achieve two objectives. First, it outlines the theoretical debate on prisoners' victimisation. Second, it presents findings from a large-scale survey which was conducted in 13 Flemish prisons. In this study we examined various types of victimisation, that is, emotional, material, physical and sexual victimisation. Bivariate findings and multivariate regression analyses are presented to gain insights into the different risk factors associated with each type of victimisation and to explore their theoretical explanations.

E. Goossens (✉) · T. Daems
Leuven Institute of Criminology (LINC), KU Leuven, Leuven, Belgium
e-mail: elien.goossens@kuleuven.be

T. Daems
e-mail: tom.daems@kuleuven.be

2 Theoretical Background

In their important study *Understanding and reducing prison violence: An integrated social control-opportunity perspective*, Steiner and Wooldredge (2020) introduced a "social control-opportunity framework" as theoretical foundation for understanding prison violence. What sets this framework apart is its comprehensive nature, as it not only incorporates the classical concepts of deprivation (Sykes, 1958; Goffman, 1961) and importation (Irwin & Cressey, 1962) but also integrates ideas from lifestyle theory (Hindelang et al., 1978), opportunity theories of crime (or social control/guardianship) (Cohen & Felson, 1979; Hirschi, 1969; Schreck, 1999), as well as victimological theories on target vulnerability and target antagonism (Finkelhor & Asdigian, 1996).

2.1 Theoretical Concepts

Steiner and Wooldredge (2020) suggest that certain imported characteristics can render incarcerated persons more **vulnerable, suitable or attractive** targets for victimisation. These characteristics include attributes like mental illness, younger age, female biological sex, being in the possession of more financial resources, prior victimisation experiences and a perceived "soft" image rather than a tough image. According to the theory, perpetrators could assess a person's level of being well-embedded within the prison system based on certain characteristics, such as their prison experience and served time. This informs potential perpetrators of the suitability of the target, indicating the risks associated with victimising a well-embedded fellow incarcerated person within the hierarchy. They may also consider the perceived likelihood of defence or retaliation against victimisation, which may be lower for individuals who have been previously (successfully) victimised, female or who are not incarcerated for violent offences (Chauvenet, 2008; Crewe, 2009).

Furthermore, some imported characteristics may motivate prisoners to attack a victim for reasons of revenge or personal status enhancement within the prisoner hierarchy, which is referred to as **antagonism**. This has been observed in particular with respect to the victimisation of sex offenders in prison as their offences tend to violate the established inmate code (Crewe, 2009; Sykes & Messinger, 1960). Similar findings have been reported for property offenders, meaning that property offenders may be more often attacked than violent offenders (Caravaca-Sánchez & Wolff, 2016; Steiner & Wooldredge, 2020; Wooldredge & Steiner, 2016). It can be hypothesised that property offenders, as opposed to violent offenders, are perceived as less tough compared to their counterparts (Crewe, 2009), and consequently, that they receive less respect within the prison hierarchy.

A third concept is **lifestyle**. On the one hand, lifestyle refers to participation in structured activities that are organised by the prison. On the other hand, it is about the involvement in unsupervised or unstructured activities—which are more likely to be illegal or forbidden inside the prison (Steiner & Wooldredge, 2020). Based on opportunity theories of crime, researchers hypothesised that the degree of formal control exerted by prison staff during structured activities could reduce opportunities for victimisation (e.g. Steiner & Wooldredge, 2020). However, empirical findings (e.g. Kuo et al., 2014; Steiner & Wooldredge, 2020; Wooldredge & Steiner, 2014, 2016) refuted this. It was observed that prisoners who worked more hours and participated in educational programmes experienced higher odds of victimisation. According to Steiner and Wooldredge (2020), this unexpected finding could be attributed to the specific context of the activities. While certain programmes are organised within the prison, these are not necessarily organised with adequate staff guardianship or formal control. Instead, such activities tend to increase opportunities due to movements within the prison and interactions with fellow prisoners. Additionally, studies have reported on the victim-offender overlap which occurs not only in society but also in prison (e.g. Daquin & Daigle, 2021; Choi, 2019; Choi & Dulisse, 2021; Kuo et al., 2021; Lahm, 2009; Reyns et al., 2018; Toman, 2019 Wooldredge & Steiner, 2012, 2013, 2014).

Finally, prisons also have contextual, **guardianship and exposure**-related features that can impact on adequate supervision or surveillance. Denser prison populations and high-security environments pose challenges for staff because in such circumstances there are more prisoners under supervision and the population may be more difficult to handle.

Prisoner populations in these settings may also experience more stress and deprivation which may encourage incarcerated persons to engage in deviant behaviour (Caravaca-Sánchez et al., 2019; Steiner & Wooldredge, 2020; Wooldredge & Steiner, 2013, 2014). Moreover, certain prison units may expose individual prisoners to more (or less) motivated offenders, for example, if prisoners reside in a separate prison unit for repeat offenders, a disciplinary unit or a unit for prisoners suffering from mental illness, where people may act more dangerously as a consequence of their mental health (Wooldredge & Steiner, 2013, 2014).

2.2 Theoretical Application to Victimisation Types

Although the abovementioned concepts have been discussed in a number of studies, few have investigated which concepts correlate with specific victimisation types. An exception is the study by Wooldredge and Steiner (2014), which compared the risk factors of assault and theft in US prisons. The researchers observed that target antagonism, and misbehaviour, better explained violent victimisation. Thus, violent victimisation was more related to a prisoner's position in the prison hierarchy and less to background characteristics. In contrast, theft was more related to a person's vulnerability based on the worth of his property (attractive/suitable target) and risks to retaliate. However, the measurements in this study were fairly limited: physical and material victimisation can consist of more than just assault and theft (e.g. fights without or with a weapon, vandalism …). Additionally, patterns of emotional and sexual victimisation were not studied.

In preparation for our empirical study on victimisation in Flemish prisons, a systematic literature review was conducted to establish a preliminary classification (Goossens et al., 2023). This review aligned with the findings of Wooldredge and Steiner (2014), indicating that physical victimisation is primarily driven by antagonism, a finding that is supported by the majority of studies included in the review. Most included studies revealed a correlation between physical victimisation and prison experience, suggesting that more experienced prisoners become targets of physical violence to elevate the status of others within the prison hierarchy. Additionally, the literature indicated a relationship between misconduct and physical victimisation, which can be attributed to lifestyle factors but also mutual provocation and antagonism. Moreover, the review did not find a clear association between antagonism and sexual victimisation. Sexual victimisation predominantly appeared to be related to vulnerability characteristics such as being female or having a history of childhood trauma. In the majority of studies no significant connections were found between sexual victimisation and factors like "antagonising" prison experience or being convicted or suspected of sex offences (Goossens et al., 2023). Vulnerability/suitability characteristics, such as higher education (as they may indicate less connection with incarcerated peers without higher education), also seemed to play a significant role with respect to emotional victimisation. Material victimisation, however, could not be that easily related to specific concepts. Indeed, our review demonstrated that both vulnerability and antagonism-related characteristics were associated with material victimisation.

It is important to note that the systematic review was primarily based on studies from the US due to the limited number of studies from other countries that could be included in the review. Furthermore, there was a lack of studies on emotional and material victimisation, making it difficult to draw definitive conclusions. Consequently, the findings of the review and the gaps that we identified in the literature offered inspiration for the design of our empirical study on prisoner-on-prisoner emotional, material, physical and sexual victimisation in Flemish prisons. In the remainder of this chapter we will discuss the background and the findings of this study.

3   The Prison System

At the start of the empirical study (2021), there were 35 prisons in Belgium. Seventeen of these prisons were located in Flanders. On 1 January 2022, the total prison population in Flanders was 5313. There are both prisons for convicts and detention centres for pre-trial prisoners but this distinction is rather theoretical as most prisons house both convicts and remand prisoners. Prison regimes vary in degree of rigour and hours that can be spent outside the cell, with the least freedom for prisoners in closed regimes and semi-open and open regimes offering more freedom. Housing is generally based on people's place of residence. Furthermore, some prisons were built quite recently, at the start of the twenty-first century, whereas other prisons date back to the second half of the nineteenth century. Some prisons face serious problems of overcrowding which implies that prisoners have to share cells and have less access to work or other activities (see e.g. CPT, 2022).

For our study we obtained permission to collect data in 13 Flemish prisons. In one prison, the study could not be conducted because of a temporary closure and the transfer of people to other institutions. In another prison, the vast majority of incarcerated persons did not meet the inclusion criteria (e.g. under 18 years of age) or stayed only briefly in the institution. The remaining two prisons refused to participate because of understaffing and organisational workload. Moreover, it should be noted that COVID-19 during the time of data collection complicated the study to a certain extent. For example, Belgian prisons faced restrictions regarding the continuation of prison-organised group activities (with the exception of walks and work) (Goossens et al., 2023), while programme participation was one of the measured variables. Due to these constraints, the research team waited until the pandemic was largely over and prison life had returned to as normal as possible. Nonetheless, unexpected prison "lockdowns" and/or stricter regulations still occurred in some facilities depending on the flow of the pandemic. Consequently, respondent recruitment methods originally planned for face-to-face interactions were at times modified to minimise contact between incarcerated persons and researchers (see Sect. 4.1 on Sampling Procedures).

4 Method

The study was evaluated by the Social and Societal Ethics Committee of KU Leuven (SMEC), which confirmed its compliance with the ethical standards in scientific research. Furthermore, the Privacy and Ethics team at KU Leuven conducted an assessment, affirming that the processing of personal data adhered to the provisions of the General Data Protection Regulation (GDPR). Data collection took place between September 2021 and September 2022.

4.1 Sampling Procedures

The study population consisted of all adult (18 +) and literate Dutch-, French- and/or English-speaking incarcerated persons, residing in a Flemish prison at the time of data collection. Excluded were those with a mental health vulnerability or individuals with the status of "internee" due to mental health issues that are related to their crimes. A potentially low response rate was expected beforehand, as the research took place in prison and dealt with sensitive questions (*cf*. victimisation), which could discourage people from participating or cause them to drop out. For example, Wolff and Shi (2009) found that response rates in similar studies ranged from 25 to 69%. In addition, Flanders has a number of smaller prisons. Drawing a random sample from these could lead to prisoners feeling excluded. Because of the aforementioned reasons, a total population sampling strategy was chosen—similar to the large-scale Dutch "Prison Project" (Dirkzwager et al., 2018). This meant that, as far as possible, all prisoners in the 13 Flemish institutions were invited to participate. To this end, a research team visited the prisons in person and handed out questionnaires at the cell doors.

Response rates, calculated on the total prison population at the time of data collection, varied between 6.2% and 48.2% with an overall response rate of 21.94%. Since these response rates are calculated on the total populations per prison, the actual rates may be slightly higher. In practice, not every single person could be approached (e.g. persons who were ill, who had a permit to leave the prison on the days of data collection, who were in isolation, ...). Lower rates (that is, 6.2% and 13.5%) were found in two prisons where alternative data collection methods[1]

---

[1] Due to COVID-19 restrictions and workload among prison staff, personal recruitment could not (fully) take place in these prisons. An alternative method of data collection involved prison staff distributing the questionnaire and retrieving them through an enclosed mailbox on the

had to be applied, in addition to two prisons for pre-trial detainees (that is, 10.3% and 12.8%).[2]

4.2 Instrument

The questionnaire was a self-report survey on prisoner-on-prisoner victimisation and fear of victimisation (which was measured as being concerned) called the *Detention monitor*.[3] The instrument was self-designed, based on an exhaustive literature review and review of existing instruments. Prior to the empirical study, a pilot study was conducted in one correctional facility, which was complemented by eight "Think aloud" interviews where incarcerated persons provided feedback on the instrument. After this phase, the survey was revised.

Prisoners were invited to report their experiences from the past two months in their current prison. The survey covered four types of victimisation and concerns: emotional, material, physical and hands-on/hands-off sexual victimisation. Each type of victimisation was surveyed through behavioural items. The advantage of using behavioural items, rather than directly asking about victimisation, is that it allows events to be measured independently of participants' subjective interpretations of the meaning of victimisation (e.g. Muehlenhard et al., 2017; Rufino et al., 2013; Wolff et al., 2006, 2007). The reference period of two months was chosen to minimise effects of telescoping for incidents with presumably lower saliency in memory (e.g. verbal insults) (Clarke et al.,

---

prison wings, which was later collected by the researchers. In another approach, the research team personally distributed the questionnaire but the responses were collected via free postal mail to reduce the need for physical visits. For specific response rates per prison, refer to Table 12 in Chapter 7 of this volume.

[2] Presumably, this is due to the nature of the population in prisons for pre-trial detainees. On the one hand, persons on remand change prison wards and prisons more often or are released more quickly than convicts. As a result, even within a relatively short time frame of two days, questionnaires sometimes got lost. On the other hand, it is plausible that these individuals are more focused on other issues than participating in research, as they still face an uncertain future.

[3] The survey can be consulted via: Goossens, E., & Daems, T. (2023). Detention monitor (KU Leuven). Zenodo. https://doi.org/10.5281/zenodo.10229096.

2008) and because of the nature of the study population, which is highly variable and frequently changes places of residence (Wolff et al., 2008).

Dependent Variables. *Emotional victimisation* was measured by asking the frequency of seven events: threats, humiliation, emotional blackmail (i.e. persuasion into doing tasks), exclusion, provocation, emotional abuse/exploitation (abusing trust/friendship) and slander (i.e. to cause problems with staff by spreading lies about the victim). *Material victimisation* involved five items: theft (while being absent), robbery (while being present/theft on the body), vandalism, material blackmail (i.e. persuasion into handing over possessions), fraud or financial scams. *Physical victimisation* was measured as physical attacks, which included incidents both without a weapon/object and with a weapon/object, as well as instances of physical restraint (i.e. preventing to move freely). *Sexual victimisation* included both hands-off and hands-on forms of victimisation: sexual remarks/jokes, sexual intimidation (i.e. through staring/whistling), exhibitionism, sexual blackmail (i.e. persuasion into agreeing with sexual contact), assault through touching and rape. The choice of the items was inspired by items from previous studies that used similar questions, with the aim of being as exhaustive as possible (e.g. Beck & Johnson, 2012; Braga et al., 2019; Caravaca-Sánchez & Wolff, 2018; Ireland & Power, 2009; Kerbs & Jolley, 2007; Kuo et al., 2014; Lahm, 2015; Vertommen et al., 2016; Wolff et al., 2009; Wooldredge, 1998).

Independent Variables. The independent variables were categorised under the theoretical constructs derived from our review of the literature (see *supra*). First, variables related to the **vulnerability**, attractiveness or suitability of the target were as follows: (1) *gender* (male/female), (2) *age* (≤30 years, 31–40 years, 41–50 years, 50 + years), (3) *nationality* (Belgian/Belgian with another nationality, or foreign), (4) highest level of completed *education* (no high school qualification, high school and/or vocational certificate, higher education), (5) *youth victimisation* (a sum scale ranging from 0 to 9e based on 3 statements where participants were invited to answer using options ranging from strongly disagree to strongly agree: "There was a lot of physical violence during my youth"; "There was a lot of emotional violence during my youth"; "There was a lot of sexual violence during my youth"), (6) *prior victimisation in* *prison* that occurred more than 2 months ago (a sum scale ranging from 0 to 12 based on 4 statements about prior emotional, material, physical or sexual victimisation where participants were invited to answer using options ranging from strongly disagree to strongly agree). Additionally, two variables were used to measure a "tough" image/attitude as opposed to a lesser tough image/attitude: (7) being convicted for or suspected of *violent offences* (yes/no) and (8) the hypothetical first *reaction to victimisation* ("What do you think your first response would be if a fellow prisoner were to attack you (cause a fight, steal from you, shout and swear at you)?": wait until the incident has passed, seek help from staff, seek help from fellow prisoners, talk to the offender/negotiate/make a deal, run away/hide/flee, scare off/threaten, fight back, other). Second, variables of **antagonism** were: (9) *number of imprisonments* (1 time (current detention), 2 to 3 times, more than 3 times), (10) *time served in current prison* ($\leq$ 1 year, + 1 to 3 years, + 3 to 5 years, + 5 years), (11) *detention status* (pre-trial or convicted prisoner), (12) being convicted for or suspected of *sex offences* (yes/no), (13) being convicted for or suspected of *drug offences* (yes/no). Third, **lifestyle** was measured as prisoners' involvement in illegitimate and legitimate activities. Regarding illegitimate activities, variables were as follows: (14) *drug use* and (15) *dealing* in prison (yes/no), (16) *general misconduct in prison* (yes/no on at least 1 of 3 statements: "I have sold items, food or protection to fellow prisoners", "I have had items and/or substances that are prohibited in this prison in my possession", "I have disobeyed the staff"), (17) *perpetration in prison* (yes/no on at least 1 of 4 statements: "I have destroyed or stolen items from fellow prisoners", "I have shouted and sworn at fellow prisoners, insulted or threatened them, excluded them or otherwise behaved in a hurtful manner towards them", "I have attacked fellow prisoners or started a fight with them", "I have performed unwanted sexual acts on fellow prisoners or pressured them into having sex"). Legitimate activities were measured as (18) *programme participation*, a scale ranging from 0 to 6: participation in recreational activities, usage of the library, work, participation in education programmes, going to prison walks and consulting a moral or religious consultant. A final set of variables referred to the situational context of the imprisonment and its potential impact on **guardianship and exposure to opportunities**:

(19) *sharing a prison cell* (yes/no), (20) the *prison unit* in which the prisoner lives (close nit, high security/extra care unit, drug-free/violence-free unit), (21) the *population size* of the prison during data collection (<200, 200–400, + 401 prisoners), (22) the *prison type* (pre-trial/remand prison, prison for convicted persons, mixed prison), (23) *the design* of the prison building (panopticon design, rectangle design with open squares in the middle or decentralised cross shape design) and (24) *the prison environment* (rural or urban surroundings).

4.3 Analyses

4.3.1 Two-step Procedure of Regression Analyses

In our study we adopted a two-step procedure which included both bivariate and multivariate analyses (e.g. Ellison, 2017). First, as measurement levels were low (i.e. nominal for the outcome variables and nominal/categorical for most covariates), bivariate cross-tabulations were calculated. Second, in accordance with the parsimony principle for model building (Kleinbaum & Klein, 2010), it was decided which covariates to include in multivariate logistic regression models based on the examination of significant ($p \leq 0.005$) bivariate findings and theoretical considerations (e.g. adding offence types to the models for comparisons with other studies).

In multivariate regression models, the models are incrementally extended with new blocks of covariates to study model improvements in the prediction of victimisation (Mortelmans, 2010). In this way, the effect of covariates on victimisation can be studied while keeping other covariates constant. Theoretically, it also informs us about the value and usefulness of model extensions, as the stepwise addition of covariate blocks was theory-based.

Conducting regression analysis in different orders can be useful to assess whether the sequence of variables impacts the results. To account for the order in which the stepwise model was constructed, the analyses were conducted in two different orders. In the first order, Block 1 included the covariates of target suitability or vulnerability. Block 2 added antagonistic and lifestyle covariates and Block 3 guardianship and exposure covariates. The final model, including Block 4, was developed to control for the effect of victimisation concerns and other victimisation types.[4] In contrast, the second regression order started with victimisation concerns and other victimisation types in the first block. Notably, no significant changes were observed in the results between the two regression orders. Consequently, the results obtained from the second regression order will be presented, as this order clarifies the role of theoretical constructs (vulnerability, guardianship, etc.) *in addition to* other victimisation types and concerns (*cf.* block 1).

4.3.2 Missing Data

There were missing data for almost all of the independent variables. However, the percentage of missing cases was below 5% for almost all variables. Data imputation was not applied due to the potential bias and uncertainty it introduces (Maltz & Targonski, 2002). Instead, we undertook a complete case analysis, assuming that the missing data were Missing At Random (MAR), meaning that the incompleteness of data was dependent on other variables but not on the missing variable itself (Allison, 2001). As a result, the sample size in the multivariate analyses on risk factors reduced to 484. Given that sample sizes impact the detection of statistical significance, which is often considered less valuable than effect sizes in terms of providing practical insights, additional attention is paid to the magnitude of odds ratios (ORs).

4.3.3 Assumptions

Before conducting the (multivariate) analyses, the dataset was inspected and several assumptions were examined. First, there was no evidence of

---

[4] Other types of victimisation (e.g. physical, sexual and material victimisation) were added as covariates to isolate and examine the relationships between the outcome variable (e.g. emotional victimisation) and the dependent variables under study (blocks 1–3), while accounting for the potential influence of these other victimisation types. Essentially, it helped the researchers to assess the specific effect of the independent variables of interest by statistically adjusting for the effects of the other victimisation types.

multicollinearity among covariates (variance inflation factors < 5 and tolerance > 0.1). Second, outliers were present in the data. Outliers are values that fall outside the typical response pattern of respondents (Mortelmans, 2010). Since the cause of the outliers was difficult to determine, it was decided not to remove the cases. Finally, the researchers paid attention to separation in the data (Mortelmans, 2010). This refers to the ratio of observations to (categories of) variables in the model (Tabachnick et al., 2019). For example, there was a particularly small number of female prisoners who had experienced physical victimisation (N = 4), which can result in an overfitted model that presents significant findings that are not generalisable. We controlled for overfitting by grouping cases into the largest possible categories and inspected the logistic outcome for unusually large standard errors and odds ratios. In the results section, the reader is warned for small sample categories and more uncertain results (e.g. which is the case for findings on gender).

5 Results

5.1 Sample and Population Parameters

As of January 1, 2022, there were 5,313 incarcerated persons in Flanders, with 94.2% being male and 5.8% female. The average age was 38 years. 58.9% had the Belgian nationality and 40.6% had a foreign nationality (0.7% was unknown). In terms of legal status, 51.8% were convicted, 39.6% were pre-trial individuals and the remaining 8.5% comprised internees and other statuses.

927 individuals completed the questionnaire with voluntary informed consent. The mean age of the sample was 41.12 (SD = 13.5) with an age range between 18 and 86 years. 863 (93%) were male and 64 (7%) female. 672 (72.5%) had the Belgian nationality and 243 (26.2%) a foreign nationality. 73.7% was convicted, awaited the outcome of an appeal or were in prison because of a revocation of a conditional release. 26.3% were pre-trial individuals. The majority had been convicted or suspected of a violent crime (violence, property crimes involving violence, terrorism, human trafficking, etc.) (39.3%). 31.2% were in

prison for drug offences, 12.9% for sexual offences, 12.2% for a property crime without violence (vandalism, theft, fraud, money laundering, etc.) and 4.3% for other offences (traffic offences, possession of weapons, prostitution, etc.). Consequently, the study sample lacks representation of people with a foreign nationality and pre-trial status, indicating that the findings primarily apply to convicted individuals with Belgian nationality in Flemish prisons.

For the reduced sample of 484, age, gender and type of crime did not differ that much. However, there were differences with regard to nationality and detention status, as the proportion of respondents with Belgian nationality increased and the proportion of pre-trial prisoners decreased. The mean age was 40.60 (SD = 12.7) with an age range between 18 and 86 years. 446 (92%) were male and 38 (8%) female. 373 (77%) had the Belgian and 111 (23%) a foreign nationality. 77.3% was convicted, awaited the outcome of an appeal or were in prison because of a revocation of a conditional release and 22.7% were pre-trial individuals. The majority had been convicted or suspected of a violent crime (39%). 31.8% were in prison for drug offences, 14% for sexual offences, 11.4% for a property crime without violence and 3.7% for other offences.

5.2   Prevalence Rates

The most frequently reported form of victimisation was emotional victimisation. 65% of the respondents expressed having experienced at least one form of emotional victimisation in the past two months in their current prison. 30% had experienced material victimisation. Physical and sexual victimisation were mentioned by 18% and 17%, respectively. Tables 1, 2, 3 and 4 offer further details on victimisation incidents.

Despite relatively high prevalence rates, most incarcerated individuals (66% of 910 persons who completed the question) expressed no victimisation concerns. 85% of prisoners who indicated that they were concerned (34%), reported feeling concerned about physical victimisation, followed by 81% being concerned about emotional victimisation, 66% about material victimisation and 10% about sexual victimisation.

Table 1 Frequencies and prevalence rates of emotional victimisation (N = 884)

Incident	Never (%)	1–2 times (%)	3–5 times (%)	≥ 6 times (%)	Victim (%)
A fellow prisoner pretended to be my friend and took advantage of this	560 (63,3)	217 (24,5)	65 (7,4)	42 (4,8)	324 (37)
A fellow prisoner threatened me, frightened me or tried to do so	582 (65,8)	216 (24,4)	48 (5,4)	38 (4,3)	302 (34)
A fellow prisoner insulted me, mocked me, humiliated me or spread gossip about me	495 (56,0)	245 (27,7)	71 (8,0)	73 (8,3)	389 (44)
A fellow inmate put pressure on me to make me do something I did not want to do, or I did so in return for protection	776 (87,8)	58 (6,6)	27 (3,1)	23 (2,6)	108 (12)
A fellow inmate excluded me, ignored me and/or encouraged others to turn against me	645 (73,0)	135 (15,3)	51 (5,8)	53 (6,0)	239 (27)

(continued)

Table 1 (continued)

Incident	Never (%)	1–2 times (%)	3–5 times (%)	≥ 6 times (%)	Victim (%)
A fellow inmate made me angry, challenged me or tried to do so	440 (49,8)	292 (33,0)	81 (9,2)	71 (8,0)	444 (50)
A fellow inmate lied about me to the staff to get me into trouble	610 (69)	171 (19,3)	51 (5,8)	52 (5,9)	274 (31)
				Overall	578 (65)

5.3 Bivariate Analyses

30 independent variables were examined (for theoretical reasons and in-depth analysis, some scale-variables were analysed as dichotomous variables, such as participation in legitimate activities). For 16 of these variables there was a significant association with at least one type of victimisation. These variables mainly relate to personal and detention backgrounds of the respondents. Contextual variables related to the prison, such as the size of the prisoner population and prison architecture, generally did not correlate with forms of victimisation. However, sharing a cell was positively associated with material victimisation (Pearson $\chi 2 = 8.711$, $p = 0.003$, phi $= 0.139$). 40% of individuals in shared cells reported material victimisation compared to 26% of prisoners in single cells.

A recurring finding is the positive association between perpetration and three types of victimisation: emotional victimisation (91% perpetrator *and* victim vs. 66% non-perpetrator and victim; Continuity correction $= 23.422$, $p < 0.001$, phi $= 0.220$), material victimisation (44% perpetrator *and* victim vs. 31% non-perpetrator and victim; Continuity correction $= 5.868$; $p = 0.015$; phi $= 0.116$) and physical

Table 2 Frequencies and prevalence rates of material victimisation (N = 896)

Incident	Never (%)	1–2 times (%)	3–5 times (%)	≥ 6 times (%)	Victim (%)
A fellow inmate put pressure on me to give away my personal belongings, medication or other items, or I did so in return for protection	808 (90,2)	57 (6,4)	13 (1,5)	18 (2,0)	88 (10)
A fellow inmate stole my personal belongings, medication or other items while I was not there	709 (79,0)	129 (14,4)	33 (3,7)	25 (2,8)	187 (21)
A fellow inmate lied to me, causing me to lose my personal belongings, medication or other items	747 (83,4)	102 (11,4)	27 (3,0)	20 (2,2)	149 (17)
A fellow inmate destroyed my personal belongings, medication or other items	810 (90,4)	60 (6,7)	14 (1,6)	12 (1,3)	86 (10)

(continued)

Table 2 (continued)

Incident	Never (%)	1–2 times (%)	3–5 times (%)	≥ 6 times (%)	Victim (%)
A fellow inmate stole my personal belongings, medication or other items while I was there	813 (90,7)	65 (7,3)	3 (0,3)	15 (1,7)	83 (9,3)
				Overall	269 (30)

Table 3 Frequencies and prevalence rates of physical victimisation (N = 901)

Incident	Never (%)	1–2 times (%)	3–5 times (%)	≥ 6 times (%)	Victim (%)
A fellow inmate attacked me without a weapon or object	754 (83,7)	109 (12,1)	26 (2,9)	12 (1,3)	147 (17)
A fellow inmate held me against my will or restrained me, locked me up or tried to do so	866 (96,1)	21 (2,3)	8 (0,9)	6 (0,7)	35 (4)
A fellow inmate attacked me with a weapon or object	843 (93,6)	39 (4,3)	10 (1,11)	9 (1,0)	58 (6)
				Overall	163 (18)

victimisation (37% perpetrator *and* victim vs. 13% non-perpetrator and victim; Continuity correction = 30.132, p < 0.001, phi = 0.256).

Similarly, there were positive associations between youth victimisation and prior victimisation in prison (occurring more than 2 months ago) and all types of victimisation. Specifically, 81% of prisoners who reported

Table 4 Frequencies and prevalence rates of sexual victimisation (N = 897)

Incident	Never (%)	1–2 times (%)	3–5 times (%)	≥ 6 times (%)	Victim (%)
A fellow inmate made sexual comments, jokes or notes that made me feel uncomfortable	790 (88)	74 (8,2)	17 (1,9)	16 (1,8)	107 (12)
A fellow inmate put pressure on me to perform sexual acts, or I did so in return for protection	882 (98,3)	6 (0,7)	5 (0,6)	4 (0,4)	15 (2)
A fellow inmate exposed their body or genitals against my wishes, or forced me to watch nude images	859 (95,8)	21 (2,3)	7 (0,8)	10 (1,1)	38 (4)
A fellow inmate looked at me or whistled at me in a way that made me feel uncomfortable	823 (91,8)	52 (5,8)	11 (1,2)	11 (1,2)	74 (8)
A fellow inmate raped me (orally, anally or vaginally)	885 (98,7)	5 (0,6)	2 (0,2)	5 (0,6)	12 (1)
A fellow inmate touched me in a way that made me feel uncomfortable	836 (93,2)	46 (5,1)	4 (0,4)	11 (1,2)	61 (7)
				Overall	157 (17)

experiencing victimisation during their youth also experienced emotional victimisation in prison, compared to 62% of those without a history of youth victimisation (Continuity correction = 21,087, p < 0.001, phi = 0.213). Furthermore, 95% of prisoners who were victimised in prison more than 2 months ago also experienced emotional victimisation in the past two months, compared to 67% of prisoners who had not been previously victimised (Continuity correction = 22.378, p < 0.001, phi = 0.221). Regarding material victimisation, the rates were 40% vs. 28% for those with and without youth victimisation, respectively (Continuity correction = 7.618, p = 0.006, phi = 0.130), and 56% vs. 30% for those with and without prior prison victimisation (Continuity correction = 18.635, p < 0.001, phi = 0.202). In terms of physical victimisation, the rates were 23% vs. 13% for those with and without youth victimisation, respectively (Continuity correction = 6,442, p = 0,011, phi = 0.121), and 53% vs. 12% for those with and without prior prison victimisation (Continuity correction = 72.445, p < 0.001, phi = 0.394). Last, for sexual victimisation, the rates were 26% vs. 15% for those with and without youth victimisation, respectively (Continuity correction = 8.454, p = 0.004, phi = 0.137), and 49% vs. 15% for those with and without prior prison victimisation (Continuity correction = 45.383, p < 0.001, phi = 0.313).

Regarding organised prison activities, there were several associations. First, there was a positive association between reporting the use of the prison library and experiencing emotional victimisation, with 75% of individuals who used the library reporting emotional victimisation, compared to 63% of those who did not use the library (Continuity correction = 5.594, p = 0.018, phi = 0.113). Second, among prisoners who took part in prison walks, 31% reported experiencing material victimisation, while this percentage was 43 for those who did not participate in prison walks (Continuity correction = 4.243, p = 0.039, phi = 0.099). No significant associations were found between specific prison activities and physical victimisation, indicating that participation in those activities did not have a notable impact on physical victimisation. Last, engaging in prison work and use of the prison library were positively associated with sexual victimisation. Specifically, 25% of prisoners with prison work reported sexual victimisation, in contrast to

14% of prisoners without prison work (Continuity correction = 8.534, p = 0.003, phi = 0.138). For the use of the prison library, this was 22.5% versus 14.1% (Continuity correction = 3.939, p = 0.047, Phi = 0.096).[5]

5.4 Multivariate Analyses

In general, the multivariate logistic models showed significant improvement after including new blocks of covariates. However, when it comes to emotional victimisation, the addition of guardianship and exposure covariates did not lead to an improvement in the prediction model ($\chi 2$ = 3.928, df = 4, p = 0.416). Similarly, for physical victimisation, the inclusion of guardianship and exposure covariates did not result in any improvements ($\chi 2$ = 0.530, df = 4, p = 0.971).

For material victimisation, the model showed improvement when guardianship and exposure covariates were added alongside the victimisation/concerns block ($\chi 2$ = 19.257, df = 4, p < 0.001). In contrast to other types of victimisation, the inclusion of antagonism/lifestyle covariates ($\chi 2$ = 8.238, df = 7, p = 0.312) and vulnerability covariates ($\chi 2$ = 15.902, df = 16, p = 0.460) did not contribute significantly to the prediction. In terms of sexual victimisation, the prediction model showed improvement with the addition of each block of covariates.

The Nagelkerke R^2 in model 1 relative to model 4 increased for emotional victimisation from 0.321 to 0.485, for material victimisation from 0.324 to 0.415, for physical victimisation from 0.384 to 0.571 and for sexual victimisation from 0.260 to 0.419. This suggests improvements in the final models over the initial models for all types of victimisation. Table 8 provides an overview of the covariate effects on the victimisation types from the final models (i.e. the models including all blocks).

---

[5] Other detailed bivariate findings can be requested from the authors.

5.4.1 Victimisation and Victimisation Concerns

Prisoners who report feeling concerned about victimisation in the past 2 months have higher odds of experiencing each type of victimisation, except for sexual victimisation where no association between concerns and victimisation is observed (OR = 0.966). The effects are strongest for emotional victimisation (OR = 8.659, 95% CI: 3.237–23.163, $p < 0.001$) and physical victimisation (OR = 6.269, 95% CI: 2.707–14.518, $p < 0.001$). Furthermore, there is an association between victimisation of one type and victimisation of another type. The strongest effect is observed for sexual victimisation, which is associated with higher odds of emotional victimisation (OR = 4.164, 95% CI: 1.417–12.238, $p = 0.010$) (Table 5).

5.4.2 Guardianship and Exposure

Based on the aforementioned analysis of model improvements, covariates related to the effectiveness of guardianship and exposure to fellow prisoners are significant for material and sexual victimisation. However, there is a non-significant decrease in the ORs of physical victimisation for prisoners residing in drug-free or violence-free units compared to those in standard prison units (OR = 0.469, 95% CI: 0.155–1.425, $p = 0.182$). The same applies to material victimisation (OR = 0.457, 95% CI: 0.194–1.075, $p = 0.073$).

Furthermore, the ORs of experiencing sexual victimisation are 2.513 times higher for prisoners in an open door regime compared to those in a closed door regime (95% CI: 1.300–4.858, $p = 0.006$). Conversely, a non-significant (but larger) effect on sexual victimisation is observed for prisoners residing in high-security or extra care units, as they exhibit decreased ORs compared to those in standard prison units (OR = 0.447, 95% CI: 0.100–1.992, $p = 0.291$). Regarding material victimisation, a

Table 5 Overview of ORs in final multivariate logistic regression model for each type of victimisation

	EV	MV	PV	SV
Block 1. Victimisation and concerns (control variables)				
Concerns (ref. no)				
Yes	8,659***	3,951***	6,269***	0,966
Emotional victimisation (ref. no)				
Yes	NA	1,792	1,673	3,864**
Material victimisation (ref. no)				
Yes	1,912	NA	2,434**	2,838***
Physical victimisation (ref. no)				
Yes	1,464	2,205**	NA	2,059
Sexual victimisation (ref. no)				
Yes	4,164**	2,689**	2,071	NA
Block 2. Guardianship and exposure				
Opportunities and less (efficient) supervision				
Shared cell (ref. no)				
Yes	0,935	2,430**	1,385	0,988
Exposure to potential motivated offenders				
Individual regime (ref. closed)				
Open	1,621	1,226	1,101	2,513**
Section/wing type (ref. standard)				
High security, extra care	0,682	0,626	0,619	0,447
Drug-free, violence-free	0,527	0,457	0,469	0,675
Block 3. Target antagonism and lifestyle				
Profile of prisoner				
Sex offender (ref. no)				
Yes	1,712	0,604	0,499	1,104

(continued)

Table 5 (continued)

	EV	MV	PV	SV
Status (ref. pre-trial)				
Convicted	1,589	1,003	2,418	0,573
Illegitimate activities				
Drug use (ref. no)				
Yes	1,633	1,107	1,435	0,401*
Drug dealing (ref. no)				
Yes	1,706	2,642*	2,136	1,778
Misconduct (ref. no)				
Yes	0,641	1,243	0,853	2,220*
Perpetration (ref. no)				
Yes	5,958***	0,900	4,238***	0,689
Legitimate activities				
Participation (scale 0–6)	1,215*	0,915	1,342**	1,156
Block 4. Target suitability/vulnerability				
Background				
Gender (ref. male)				
Female	0,996	0,964	0,047**	2,503
Age (ref. ≤ 30 years)				
31–40 years	0,867	0,878	0,685	0,969
41–50 years	0,878	1,606	0,600	1,721
50 + years	0,571	1,294	0,444	1,405
Education (ref. < high school)				
High school and/or vocational certificate	1,545	1,318	1,345	0,821
Higher education	2,331	0,911	2,693	1,248
History of victimisation				
Youth victimisation (scale 0 – 9)	1,229***	1,075	0,979	1,025
Prison victimisation > 2 months (scale 0 – 12)	1,607**	1,126	1,492***	1,376***

(continued)

Table 5 (continued)

	EV	MV	PV	SV
Toughness				
Violent offender (ref. no)				
Yes	0,703	0,825	1,181	0,624
Reaction to hypothetical violence (ref. wait (endure))				
Seek help; staff	0,253*	1,327	0,319	1,686
Seek help; prisoners	0,577	0,621	2,345	1,181
Make a deal	0,933	1,662	0,307	2,408
Run away, hide, flee	0,319	0,517	0,768	1,170
Scare off (threaten)	2,840	0,602	0,067	3,391
Fight back	0,636	1,488	0,353	1,620
Other or combination	0,324	1,964	0,317	2,160
χ^2-test	$\chi^2 = 41,991$; $p < 0,001$	$\chi^2 = 15,902$; $p = 0,460$	$\chi^2 = 45,301$; $p < 0,001$	$\chi^2 = 30,640$; $p = 0,015$
Goodness of fit (Hosmer and Lemeshow)	$\chi^2 = 4,407$; $p = 0,819$	$\chi^2 = 7,327$; $p = 0,502$	$\chi^2 = 14,048$; $p = 0,081$	$\chi^2 = 8,044$; $p = 0,429$
Cox & Snell R^2 (Nagelkerke R^2)	0,339 (0,485)	0,299 (0,415)	0,349 (0,571)	0,265 (0,419)
% Classification correct	79,5	77,9	89,3	85,5

MV = Material victimisation; EV = Emotional victimisation; PV = Physical victimisation; SV = Sexual victimisation; NA = Not applicable.
*$p \leq 0.05$; $p \leq 0.01$**; ***$p \leq 0.001$; Large effect, not significant

strong positive association is found between sharing a prison cell and experiencing victimisation (OR = 2.430, 95% CI: 1.360–4.342, p = 0.003).

5.4.3 Target Antagonism and Lifestyle

Most effects of antagonistic and lifestyle-related covariates are found for physical victimisation. First, there is a significant association between participation in prison-organised activities and physical victimisation: for each 1-unit increase on the 6-point scale of activities, the ORs of physical victimisation increase by 1.342 (95% CI: 1.064–1.692, p = 0.013). Second, there is also a significant increase in ORs when prisoners report being perpetrators themselves during detention compared to those who do not report this (OR = 4.238, 95% CI: 1.785–10.060, p = 0.001). Third, there is a non-significant effect of involvement in drug dealing in prison on physical victimisation, with ORs increasing by 2.136 (95% CI: 0.566–8.053, p = 0.262). Last, a non-significant positive effect on physical victimisation is observed for convicted individuals compared to pre-trial prisoners (OR = 2.418, 95% CI: 0.886–6.597, p = 0.085).

The significant association between victimisation and perpetration reoccurs in the case of emotional victimisation (OR = 5.958, 95% CI: 2.477–14.327, p < 0.001). For sexual victimisation, there is no association with person-directed perpetration (OR = 0.689, 95% CI: 0.318–1.494, p = 0.345), but there is an association with engaging in general rule-breaking behaviours or misconduct (OR = 2.220, 95% CI: 1.096–4.494, p = 0.027). However, the victim-perpetrator (or misconduct) overlap does not emerge in the case of material victimisation (OR = 0.900, 95% CI: 0.468–1.730, p = 0.752 and OR = 1.243, 95% CI: 0.669–2.311, p = 0.492).

Furthermore, similar to physical victimisation, (non-significant) positive effects of drug dealing are found on emotional (OR = 1.706, 95% CI: 0.464–6.271, p = 0.421) and sexual (OR = 1.778, 95% CI: 0.574–5.505, p = 0.319) victimisation. In contrast to perpetration and misconduct, a significant relationship between drug dealing and material victimisation was observed. Prisoners who reported involvement in drug dealing had 2.642 times higher odds of experiencing material victimisation (95% CI: 1.003–6.957, p = 0.049) compared to those who did not engage in drug dealing within the prison setting. Additionally, there appears to be a small non-significant effect of drug use in prison on emotional victimisation (OR = 1.633, 95% CI: 0.768–3.472, p =

0.203). Interestingly, this effect reverses for sexual victimisation, where drug use is associated with a significant *decrease* in ORs (OR = 0.401, 95% CI: 0.179–0.902, p = 0.027). However, these findings should be interpreted with caution considering the results of the bivariate analyses. Although the effect was also observed in the multivariate model with a different order, there was no significant association between drug use and sexual victimisation in the cross-tabulations. The cross-tabulations indicated a negligible association (Continuity correction = 0.808, p = 0.369, Phi = 0.046).

Regarding the legitimate lifestyle, it was found that engaging in prison-organised activities is significantly associated with emotional victimisation, in addition to physical victimisation. More specifically, for each unit increase on the scale, there was a 1.215 increase in the odds of experiencing emotional victimisation (95% CI: 1.005–1.468, p = 0.044).

Last, there seems to be a positive effect on emotional victimisation of having committed, or being suspected of, sexual offences compared to prisoners who did not report sexual offences, but this association is not significant (OR = 1.712, 95% CI: 0.696–4.211, p = 0.241).

5.4.4 Target Suitability and Vulnerability

Previous victimisation is particularly correlated with emotional victimisation. For instance, for each 1-unit increase on the scale of past victimisation experienced in prison (i.e. more than 2 months ago), the emotional victimisation odds increase by 1.607 (95% CI: 1.138–2.268, p = 0.007). Additionally, an increase on the scale of childhood victimisation is also associated with an increase in emotional victimisation odds (OR = 1.229, 95% CI: 1.094–1.380, p < 0.001). However, these associations are not observed for other types of victimisation. Only previous victimisation in prison is positively associated with physical victimisation (OR = 1.492, 95% CI: 1.212–1.838, p < 0.001) and sexual victimisation (OR = 1.376, 95% CI: 1.159–1.634, p < 0.001).

Regarding the other background covariates, findings on the effect of age are mixed, although there are no significant relationships observed.

First, slightly increased odds for material victimisation are observed for prisoners in the age range of 41–50 years compared to prisoners aged 30 years or younger (OR = 1.606, 95% CI: 0.775–1.080, p = 0.292). Prisoners in this age range also experience increased odds for sexual victimisation (OR = 1.721, 95% CI: 0.722–4.104, p = 0.221). In contrast, prisoners aged 50 years or older report decreased odds for physical victimisation (OR = 0.444, 95% CI: 0.127–1.551, p = 0.203).

Turning to education, no significant associations are found. However, notable effects can be observed. Prisoners with a high school and/or vocational certificate have slightly increased odds of experiencing emotional victimisation compared to those without a high school degree (OR = 1.545, 95% CI: 0.897–2.662, p = 0.117). Furthermore, prisoners with a higher education show even stronger effects, with a 2.331 increase in emotional victimisation odds (95% CI: 0.902–6.023, p = 0.080) and a 2.693 increase in physical victimisation odds (95% CI: 0.828–8.759, p = 0.100).

Regarding gender, the model reveals a significant association for two victimisation types. Specifically, being female as opposed to being male, was associated with decreased odds of experiencing physical victimisation (OR = 0.047, 95% CI: 0.006–0.351, p = 0.003), but increased odds of experiencing sexual victimisation (OR = 2.503, 95% CI: 0.896–6.990, p = 0.080). However, it is important to note that the number of women included in the multivariate analysis was small, with only 4 out of 38 reporting physical victimisation and 15 reporting sexual victimisation. The limited sample size of these groups can introduce uncertainty in the findings.

Similarly, findings regarding reported responses to hypothetical victimisation should be interpreted with caution due to small group sizes, which are reflected in wider confidence intervals as well and, consequently, less certain conclusions. In comparison to prisoners who reported no response (waiting, enduring the attack), prisoners who reported that they would seek support from fellow prisoners had increased odds of experiencing physical victimisation (N = 17, 5 physical victims) (OR = 2.345, 95% CI: 0.302–18.217, p = 0.415). All other responses were associated with non-significant decreases in the odds of physical victimisation. For emotional victimisation, prisoners who thought they would threaten and deter the offender (N = 9, 8 emotional victims) had increased odds (OR = 2.840, 95% CI: 0.201–40.211, p = 0.440), similar to sexual victimisation (N = 9, 3 sexual victims) (OR = 3.391, 95% CI: 0.395–29.128, p = 0.266). Conversely, seeking help from staff was associated with a significant decrease in the odds of emotional victimisation (N = 71, 40 emotional victims) (OR = 0.253, 95% CI: 0.067–0.952, p = 0.042), but a non-significant increase in the odds of sexual victimisation (N = 71, 11 sexual victims) (OR = 1.686, 95% CI: 0.386–7.364, p = 0.488).

It is noteworthy that responding to victimisation appears to be more often associated with increased odds for sexual and physical victimisation compared to other victimisation types. Moreover, few effects of responses are observed on material victimisation odds, except for a 1.662 increase (95% CI: 0.457–6.042, p = 0.441) when prisoners report they would negotiate or make a deal with their offender compared to those who do not respond to victimisation (N = 56, 35 material victims).

6   Discussion

This study examined the prevalence and associated risk factors of various prisoner-on-prisoner victimisation types in 13 Flemish prisons. A sample of 927 prisoners revealed that almost two-thirds (65%) experienced emotional victimisation during their detention, with humiliation (44%) and provocation (50%) being the main reported problems. The high frequency of emotional victimisation is, on the one hand, consistent with previous studies (e.g. Caravaca-Sánchez & Wolff, 2018; Edgar et al., 2003) but on the other hand, contrasts with the dominant focus on physical and sexual victimisation in the majority of past studies. The findings on provocation also point to the known victim-offender overlap (e.g. Choi, 2019; Daquin & Daigle, 2021; Kuo et al., 2021; Toman, 2019), as victims may be challenged to proceed to perpetration themselves after emotional bullying. Furthermore, physical and sexual victimisation were reported by respectively 18% and 17% of respondents in Flemish prisons. Sexual victimisation mainly involved hands-off forms of victimisation such as sexual jokes (12%) and physical victimisation predominantly prisoner-on-prisoner fights without weapon (17%). Moreover, a substantial proportion of the sample reported material victimisation (30%), which was mainly about theft of personal items that was not directly witnessed by the victim (21%). It could be that prisoners here primarily *assumed* theft, suspecting a fellow prisoner for the loss of an item. However, 17% also reported they were conned or cheated out of items, which involves a more clear and identifiable victimisation and perpetration pattern.

Regarding the risk factors, several associations that were identified in bivariate analyses were consistent with the multivariate results, indicating that these variables are risk factors independent of the influence of other variables. The victim-offender overlap applies to emotional and physical victimisation (and to sexual victimisation when it comes to misconduct) but not to material victimisation, unless in the context of a drug deal. In addition to the victim-offender overlap, there is the issue of multiple victimisation, as both bivariate and multivariate analyses indicated that one type of victimisation is associated with other types and prior prison victimisation is associated with more recent emotional, physical and sexual victimisation.

Furthermore, the results seem to indicate that participation in organised programmes is independently associated with emotional and physical victimisation. Given the multivariate associations, it appears that increased participation in activities is accompanied by an increase in victimisation opportunities (hypothetically, this could be attributed to less efficient guardianship during movements and activities). More specifically, however, it is challenging to determine differences in victimisation based on the type of activity under study. In bivariate analyses, the use of the prison library correlated with emotional and sexual victimisation (although it is also possible that prisoners who read more often, are better skilled in reporting/recognising emotional/sexual victimisation in a written survey). Regarding physical victimisation, there was no bivariate association between any specific activity and victimisation, meaning that the correlation only occurred when the scale variable—the number of activities one participated in—was included in the (multivariate) analyses.

Youth *and* prior prison victimisation were correlated with all types of victimisation in the bivariate analyses, but in the multivariate models this was only the case for emotional victimisation. However, prior prison victimisation alone was still associated with physical and sexual victimisation.

Furthermore, there are similarities, but also some differences, between the multivariate results of our empirical study and the findings from the systematic review (Goossens et al., 2023). On the one hand, characteristics related to the vulnerability or attractiveness of the target seem to be better associated with **emotional victimisation** than with other victimisation types (e.g. higher education, youth victimisation and prior prison victimisation, while only prior prison victimisation is associated with sexual/physical victimisation and findings on the association between education and physical victimisation were mixed). On the other hand, the empirical study identified additional associations for emotional victimisation that were not addressed in the systematic review, although this can be partially attributed to the limited attention of previous researchers to emotional victimisation. These include the antagonistic factors (e.g. sex offences), legitimate lifestyle factors (e.g. participation in activities) and illegitimate lifestyle factors (e.g. perpetration, drug dealing).

Regarding material victimisation, the bivariate and multivariate analyses were consistent, whereas this was less clear based on the review of international research. **Material victimisation** seems to be primarily explained by contextual factors and opportunities/exposure (higher risk when sharing a cell, lower risk in drug-free and/or violence-free prison units, higher risk when involved in drug deals). This contrasts with the study by Wooldredge and Steiner (2014), which found that theft victimisation was related to target vulnerability or attractiveness based on belongings. However, our empirical study did not include questions about financial situation or belongings in prison.

Sexual victimisation tends to be related to vulnerability in most previous studies (e.g. being female and childhood trauma) but not antagonism (Goossens et al., 2023). This is partly confirmed in our study: despite a limited number of women in the sample, being female appears to be associated with a higher risk of sexual victimisation, while being female is not associated with other types of victimisation and negatively associated with physical victimisation. Childhood victimisation was not associated with sexual victimisation in this study. However, it is worth noting that the item related to sexual childhood victimisation had the highest rate of unanswered responses compared to the other two childhood-related items. On the other hand, prior prison victimisation was found to be associated with sexual victimisation. Despite these findings on target vulnerability, it is important to note the associations found between prisoners engaged in misconduct, drug dealing and sexual victimisation. Hypothetically, these associations can reflect a lifestyle that can create both antagonism (when the lifestyle frustrates other prisoners, as in the case of a failed drug deal) and opportunities (drug deals leading to interactions with motivated offenders). It becomes clear that the concept of lifestyle is intertwined with target antagonism and opportunities.

Last, previous studies have suggested that violent or physical victimisation could be better explained by antagonism, such as due to an illegitimate lifestyle (Goossens et al., 2023; Wooldredge & Steiner, 2014). These findings are partially supported by the current study regarding **physical victimisation**, although associations regarding the illegitimate lifestyle also occur for other types of victimisation. However, there also appears to be a positive correlation between having a convicted status as opposed to pre-trial status and physical victimisation, in contrast to the findings on other types of victimisation which showed no associations. If incarcerated persons seek to enhance their status through victimising another, it is probably most effective to achieve this through visible forms of violence that can be recognised by others, such as physical violence. Hypothetically, this could explain why antagonism and other victimisation types are mostly related to triggering other persons (i.e. illegitimate lifestyle, being an offender) while antagonism and physical victimisation might also be about hierarchical status, although this should be further explored. The relationship between being a convicted individual and physical victimisation could also be attributed to reporting effects. It is possible that individuals in pre-trial detention are less inclined to report negative experiences, which may affect the observed relationship. Another factor to consider is the amount of time spent inside the cell by pre-trial individuals, which could influence the opportunities for physical victimisation. The findings on convicted persons also contrast somewhat with the cross-tabulation results for other types of victimisation: although not statistically significant, remand prisoners exhibited *slightly* higher percentages of victimisation compared to convicted detained individuals for emotional, sexual and material victimisation.

Overall, it cannot be said that one theoretical construct exclusively explains a specific type of victimisation, as risk factors for all types of victimisation exist at different levels. However, material victimisation appears to be more context-dependent compared to other types of victimisation. Additionally, there are several overlapping risk factors, such as perpetration and prior prison victimisation.

7 Study Limitations

The study has certain limitations. First, the cross-sectional design used in examining risk factors means that causal relationships cannot be assumed (Clark et al., 2021). For example, the association between concerns and victimisation can work both ways, as concerned behaviour may make someone a more appealing target to offenders, *or* being concerned could be a result of prior victimisation. Similarly, the victim-offender overlap could be explained by offenders exposing themselves to higher risks *or* victims becoming more violent to avoid further victimisation. Additionally, alternative explanations can be proposed for certain theoretical insights. For example, the association between higher education and victimisation could be attributed to a better willingness to **report incidents of victimisation** and **higher proficiency in reading and writing skills** among those with a higher education. The same applies to the strong association between prior victimisation and current victimisation, where individuals who report past victimisation may also be more inclined to report current victimisation. It is recommended to further study these different types of victimisation in prison using qualitative research methods, such as observations and interviews, to further examine the dynamic and processes of the associations we found in our quantitative study.

Second, the findings rely on self-reporting by prisoners, which presents potential drawbacks of over- or underreporting. Prisoners may feel uncomfortable disclosing their victimisation, especially in shared prison cells, or they may overreport victimisation to impact on the reputation of the prison system (e.g. Blitz et al., 2008; Caravaca-Sánchez et al., 2019). Furthermore, prisoners' responses may (un)consciously differ from the reality, which can be the case for the question on reactions against potential victimisation or when telescoping effects are at play.

Third, there are sample-related limitations. Total population sampling is not random sampling. This means that we had no control over the representativeness of the realised sample for the characteristics of the Flemish prison population (e.g. nationality, detention/legal status). The fact that fewer (significant) associations were found for contextual variables may also be related to the sample. For example, the number of prisoners in a high security and extra care unit ($N = 30$ of 927 vs 771 regular unit) was limited.

Fourth, there were missing data on the independent variables and the complete case analysis for the examination of risk factors resulted in nearly halving the sample size, thereby reducing statistical power and increasing some uncertainty in research findings (e.g. the association between being female and victimisation). On the one hand, this means that there was information loss. On the other hand, the total sample ($N = 927$) and the reduced sample ($N = 484$) did not differ that much from each other in terms of gender, age and offence types. There also seemed to be randomness present in the missing values, as the missing observations for most independent variables were below 5%. The risk of imputing erroneous data did not outweigh the loss of information.

Finally, there are two drawbacks related to the construction and translation of the questionnaire. Regarding the questions on fear of victimisation, the operationalisation as "concerns about victimisation" does not measure the full width of the experience (Farrall et al., 1997). Fear may be accompanied by a variety of emotional experiences, such as feelings of anger or revenge and cognitive processes, such as risk perceptions (Farrall & Ditton, 1999). Moreover, victim perceptions are subjective: not all individuals who objectively experience an incident identify themselves as victimised. Hence, the present study measured victimisation and fear, as a product of how it was reported (incidents and concerns), which may not fully correspond to the social reality of prison. However, it is important to emphasise that normalising certain factual incidents in prison, such as insulting others or stealing trivial items, would not contribute to the reintegration process of any prisoner. These incidents would not be accepted in social interactions outside the prison either, regardless of how the person who experienced the incidents perceives it.

References

Allison, P. D. (2001). *Missing data*. Sage.
Beck, A. J., & Johnson, C. (2012). *National Former Prisoner Survey, 2008—Sexual victimization reported by former state prisoners, 2008*. Bureau of Justice Statistics.
Blitz, C. L., Wolff, N., & Shi, J. (2008). Physical victimization in prison: The role of mental illness. *International Journal of Law and Psychiatry, 31*(5), 385–393. https://doi.org/10.1016/j.ijlp.2008.08.005
Braga, T., De Castro-Rodrigues, A., Di Folca, S. M. S., & Gonçalves, R. A. (2019). How dark are dark figures? Official and self-report rates of inmate-on-inmate victimization. *Victims & Offenders, 14*(6), 745–757. https://doi.org/10.1080/15564886.2019.1627683
Caravaca-Sánchez, F., & Wolff, N. (2016). Self-report rates of physical and sexual violence among Spanish inmates by mental illness and gender. *The Journal of Forensic Psychiatry & Psychology, 27*(3), 443–458. https://doi.org/10.1080/14789949.2016.1145721
Caravaca-Sánchez, F., & Wolff, N. (2018). Understanding polyvictimization in prison: Prevalence and predictors among men inmates in Spain. *Journal of Interpersonal Violence, 36*(7–8), 3411–3437. https://doi.org/10.1177/0886260518775751
Caravaca-Sánchez, F., Wolff, N., & Teasdale, B. (2019). Exploring associations between interpersonal violence and prison size in Spanish prisons. *Crime & Delinquency, 65*(14), 2019–2043. https://doi.org/10.1177/0011128718763134
Chauvenet, A., Rostaing, C., & Orlic, F. (2008). *La violence carcérale en question*. Presses Universitaires de France.

Choi, J. (2019). Victimization, fear of crime, procedural injustice and inmate misconduct: An application of general strain theory in South Korea. *International Journal of Law, Crime and Justice, 59*, 1–12. https://doi.org/10.1016/j.ijlcj.2019.100346

Choi, J., & Dulisse, B. (2021). Behind closed doors: The role of risky lifestyles and victimization experiences on fear of future victimization among South Korean inmates. *Journal of Interpersonal Violence, 36* (21–22), 10817–10841. https://doi.org/10.1177/0886260519888186

Clark, T., Foster, L., Sloan, L., & Bryman, A. (2021). *Bryman's social research methods.* Oxford University Press.

Clarke, P. M., Fiebig, D. G., & Gerdtham, U.-G. (2008). Optimal recall length in survey design. *Journal of Health Economics, 27* (5), 1275–1284. https://doi.org/10.1016/j.jhealeco.2008.05.012

Cohen, L. E., & Felson, M. (1979). Social change and crime rate trends: A routine activity approach. *American Sociological Review, 44*, 588–608.

CPT. (2022). Rapport au Gouvernement de Belgique relatif à la visite effectuée en Belgique par le Comité européen pour la prévention de la torture et des peines ou traitements inhumains ou dégradants (CPT) du 2 au 9 novembre 2021, CPT/Inf (2022). Council of Europe.

Crewe, B. (2009). *The prisoner society: Power, adaptation and social life in an English prison.* Oxford University Press.

Daquin, J. C., & Daigle, L. E. (2021). The victim-offender overlap in prison: Examining the factors associated with group membership. *Journal of Interpersonal Violence, 1–24,*. https://doi.org/10.1177/0886260519898427

Dirkzwager, A. J. E., Nieuwbeerta, P., Beijersbergen, K. A., Bosma, A. Q., de Cuyper, R., Doekhie, J., Eichelsheim, V., de Goede, S., van der Laan, P. H., Lamet, W., Palmen, H., Raaijmakers, E., Ramakers, A., Reef, J., van der Stelt, S., Wensveen, M., & Wermink, H. (2018). Cohort profile: The prison project—a study of criminal behavior and life circumstances before, during, and after imprisonment in the Netherlands. *Journal of developmental and life-course criminology, 4* (1), 120–135. https://doi.org/10.1007/s40865-017-0077-2

Edgar, K., Martin, C., & O'Donnell, I. (2003). *Prison violence: The dynamics of conflict, fear and power.* Willan.

Ellison, J. M. (2017). *An opportunity model of victimization risk for jail inmates and correctional officers* (PhD thesis). University of Nebraska.

Farrall, S., Bannister, J. O. N., Ditton, J., & Gilchrist, E. (1997). Questioning the measurement of the 'fear of crime': Findings from a major methodological study. *British Journal of Criminology, 37*(4), 658–679. https://doi.org/10.1093/oxfordjournals.bjc.a014203

Farrall, S., & Ditton, J. (1999). Improving the measurement of attitudinal responses: An example from a crime survey. *International Journal of Social Research Methodology, 2*(1), 55–68. https://doi.org/10.1080/136455799295186

Finkelhor, D., & Asdigian, N. L. (1996). Risk factors for youth victimization: Beyond a lifestyles/routine activities theory approach. *Violence and Victims, 11*(1), 3–19. https://doi.org/10.1891/0886-6708.11.1.3

Goffman, E. (1961). *Asylums: Essays on the social situation of mental patients and other inmates*. Penguin Books.

Goossens, E., Robert, L., & Daems, T. (2023). Individual and contextual risk factors of prisoners' victimization: A best fit framework synthesis. *Aggression and Violent Behavior, 70*. https://doi.org/10.1016/j.avb.2023.101826

Goossens, E., Maes, E., Robert, L., Daems, T., & Mertens, A. (2023). Victimization in prison. A study of victimization and prison climate dimensions in Belgian prisons. *Victims & Offenders*, 1–35. https://doi.org/10.1080/15564886.2023.2282978

Hindelang, M. J., Gottfredson, M. R., & Garofalo, J. (1978). *Victims of personal crime: An empirical foundation for a theory of personal victimization*. Ballinger.

Hirschi, T. (1969). *Causes of delinquency*. University of California Press.

Ireland, J. L., & Power, C. L. (2009). Fear of bullying among prisoners: Association with experience, psychological distress and respondent sex. *Journal of Aggression, Conflict and Peace Research, 1*(3), 22. https://doi.org/10.1108/17596599200900015

Irwin, J., & Cressey, D., R. . (1962). Thieves, convicts and the inmate culture. *Social Problems, 10*(2), 142–155. https://doi.org/10.1525/sp.1962.10.2.03a00040

Kerbs, J. J., & Jolley, J. M. (2007). Inmate-on-inmate victimization among older male prisoners. *Crime & Delinquency, 53*(2), 187–218. https://doi.org/10.1177/0011128706294119

Kleinbaum, D. G., & Klein, M. (2010). *Logistic regression. A self-learning text* (3d ed.). Springer.

Kuo, S., Cuvelier, S. J., & Huang, Y. (2014). Identifying risk factors for victimization among male prisoners in Taiwan. *International Journal of Offender*

Therapy and Comparative Criminology, 58(2), 231–257. https://doi.org/10.1177/0306624X12465272

Kuo, S.-Y., Chang, K., Chen, Y., & Lai, Y. (2021). Assessing the victim-offender overlap in prison victimization and misconduct among Taiwanese male inmates. *British Journal of Criminology, 20*, 1–22. https://doi.org/10.1093/bjc/azab066

Lahm, K. F. (2009). Physical and property victimization behind bars: A multi-level examination. *International Journal of Offender Therapy and Comparative Criminology, 53*(3), 348–365. https://doi.org/10.1177/0306624X08316504

Lahm, K. F. (2015). Predictors of violent and nonviolent victimization behind bars: An exploration of women inmates. *Women & Criminal Justice, 25*(4), 273–291. https://doi.org/10.1080/08974454.2014.989304

Maltz, M. D., & Targonski, J. (2002). A note on the use of county-level ucr data. Journal of *Quantitative Criminology, 18*(3), 297–318. https://doi.org/10.1023/A:101606002084

Mortelmans, D. (2010). *Logistische regressie*. Acco.

Muehlenhard, C. L., Peterson, Z. D., Humphreys, T. P., & Jozkowski, K. N. (2017). Evaluating the one-in-five statistic: Women's risk of sexual assault while in college. *The Journal of Sex Research, 54*(4–5), 549–576. https://doi.org/10.1080/00224499.2017.1295014

Reyns, B. W., Woo, Y., Lee, H. D., & Yoon, O. (2018). Vulnerability versus opportunity: Dissecting the role of low self-control and risky lifestyles in violent victimization risk among Korean inmates. *Crime & Delinquency, 64*(4), 423–447. https://doi.org/10.1177/0011128716679375

Rufino, K. A., Fox, K. A., Cramer, R. J., & Kercher, G. A. (2013). The gang–victimization link: Considering the effects of ethnicity and protective behaviors among prison inmates. *Deviant Behavior, 34*(1), 25–37. https://doi.org/10.1080/01639625.2012.679898

Schreck, C. J. (1999). Criminal victimization and low self-control: An extension and test of a general theory of crime. *Justice Quarterly, 16*(3), 633–654. https://doi.org/10.1080/07418829900094291

Steiner, B., & Wooldredge, J. D. (2020). *Understanding and reducing prison violence: An integrated social control-opportunity perspective*. Routledge.

Sykes, G. M. (1958). *The society of captives: A study of a maximum security prison*. Princeton University Press.

Sykes, G. M., & Messinger, S. L. (1960). The inmate social system. In R. A. Cloward, D. R. Cressey, G. H. Grosser, R. McCleery, L. E. Ohlin, G. M. Sykes, & S. L. Messinger (Eds.), *Theoretical studies in social organization of the prison* (pp. 5–19). Social Science Research Council.

Tabachnick, B. G., Fidell, L. S., & Ullman, J. B. (2019). *Using multivariate statistics*. Pearson.

Toman, E. L. (2019). The victim-offender overlap behind bars: Linking prison misconduct and victimization. *Justice Quarterly, 36*(2), 350–382. https://doi.org/10.1080/07418825.2017.1402072

Vertommen, T., Schipper-van Veldhoven, N., Wouters, K., Kampen, J. K., Brackenridge, C. H., Rhind, D. J. A., Neels, K., & Van Den Eede, F. (2016). Interpersonal violence against children in sport in the Netherlands and Belgium. *Child Abuse & Neglect, 51*, 223–236. https://doi.org/10.1016/j.chiabu.2015.10.006

Wolff, N., Blitz, C. L., Shi, J., Bachman, R., & Siegel, J. A. (2006). Sexual violence inside prisons: Rates of victimization. *Journal of Urban Health, 83*(5), 835–848. https://doi.org/10.1007/s11524-006-9065-2

Wolff, N., Blitz, C. L., Shi, J., Siegel, J., & Bachman, R. (2007). Physical violence inside prisons: Rates of victimization. *Criminal Justice and Behavior, 34*(5), 588–599. https://doi.org/10.1177/0093854806296830

Wolff, N., Shi, J., & Bachman, R. (2008). Measuring victimization inside prisons: Questioning the questions. *Journal of Interpersonal Violence, 23*(10), 1343–1362. https://doi.org/10.1177/0886260508314301

Wolff, N., & Shi, J. (2009). Feelings of safety inside prison among male inmates with different victimization experiences. *Violence and Victims, 24*(6), 800–816. https://doi.org/10.1891/0886-6708.24.6.800

Wooldredge, J. D. (1998). Inmate lifestyles and opportunities for victimization. *Journal of Research in Crime and Delinquency, 35*(4), 480–502. https://doi.org/10.1177/0022427898035004006

Wooldredge, J. D., & Steiner, B. (2012). Race group differences in prison victimization experiences. *Journal of Criminal Justice, 40*(5), 358–369. https://doi.org/10.1016/j.jcrimjus.2012.06.011

Wooldredge, J. D., & Steiner, B. (2013). Violent victimization among state prison inmates. *Violence and Victims, 28*(3), 531–551. https://doi.org/10.1891/0886-6708.11-00141

Wooldredge, J. D., & Steiner, B. (2014). A bi-level framework for understanding prisoner victimization. *Journal of Quantitative Criminology, 30*(1), 141–162. https://doi.org/10.1007/s10940-013-9197-y

Wooldredge, J. D., & Steiner, B. (2016). Assessing the need for gender-specific explanations of prisoner victimization. *Justice Quarterly, 33*(2), 209–238. https://doi.org/10.1080/07418825.2014.897364

The Victim-Offender Overlap in Prisons and Associated Challenges for Prison Managers

Esther F. J. C. van Ginneken

This book is testament to the fact that imprisonment cannot fully guarantee incapacitation: offending and victimisation do not necessarily end upon entry into prison. In-prison offending may include, for example, assaults on staff and fellow incarcerated individuals, contraband trading and even continued criminal activity that extends beyond the prison walls. An impressive body of research has developed on the predictors of offending and misconduct in prison (Baggio et al., 2020; Beijersbergen et al., 2015; Berghuis et al., 2021; Bosma et al., 2020; Camp et al., 2003; Drury & DeLisi, 2010; Gaes et al., 2002; Lahm, 2016; Logan et al., 2022; Steiner et al., 2014) and on the predictors of victimisation (Caravaca-Sánchez & Wolff, 2017; Caravaca-Sánchez et al., 2019;

This publication is part of the project 'The Social Ecology of Violence in Prisons', with project number VI.vidi.211.003 of the research program NWO Talent Program Vidi, which is financed by the Dutch Research Council (NWO).

E. F. J. C. van Ginneken (✉)
Institute for Criminal Law and Criminology, Leiden University, Leiden, The Netherlands
e-mail: e.f.j.c.van.ginneken@law.leidenuniv.nl

© The Author(s), under exclusive license to Springer Nature Switzerland AG 2024
T. Daems and E. Goossens (eds.), *Understanding Prisoner Victimisation*, Palgrave Studies in Victims and Victimology, https://doi.org/10.1007/978-3-031-54350-0_4

Goossens et al., 2023; Pérez et al., 2010; Reyns et al., 2018; Steiner et al., 2017; Wolff et al., 2009). These parallel lines of research have not been connected as well as they should be; it is often not recognised that victims may become offenders, offenders may become victims or the roles of people in an incident may be ambiguous (Edgar & O'Donnell, 1998). While offending has been considered as a predictor of victimisation in earlier work (for a review, see Steiner et al., 2017), only recently have prison researchers developed and tested specific theories about the victim-offender overlap (Daquin & Daigle, 2021; Kuo et al., 2022; Martens et al., 2021; Toman, 2019). This contribution discusses what is known about the victim-offender overlap in prisons, and how we can understand this from a theoretical point of view. It will be shown that the key to understanding the causes of violence—and the related victim-offender overlap—is the context in which it takes place: one category of assaults can be understood as an emotional or situational phenomenon, and another category of assaults can be understood as an organised and more deliberate phenomenon, linked to the illicit economy. In the second part of this chapter, the victim-offender overlap related to the second category will be examined from a prison-management perspective, using data from interviews with Dutch prison managers.

1 The Victim-Offender Overlap: Theory and Prior Research

Victims and offenders are not mutually exclusive categories; they may be related in various ways, as is summarised in Table 1. In the first situation, individuals are both victim and offender in the same incident, for example a prisoner who starts a fight may also be physically harmed in the same fight. In these cases of mutual assault, the roles of victim and offender are often ambiguous (Edgar & O'Donnell, 1998). The victimisation and offending take place in the same incident, and are therefore (nearly) simultaneous. In the second situation, the experience or threat of victimisation may be the motive for later offending, and vice versa: an act of offending may also be followed by retaliation and, thus, victimisation.

In these cases, the roles are reversed. The victimisation and offending take place in separate—but linked—incidents. In the third situation, individuals are victim and offender in separate—not linked—incidents; for example, a person assaults someone, and is victimised in an unrelated incident by someone else. In the fourth situation, offending and victimisation are tied to roles in the illicit economy; for example, a person hiding contraband in their cell (offender) is doing so under duress (victim). Thus far, little is known about explanations and predictors for these different categories of the victim-offender overlap, although we know that the overlap exists.

Traditionally, adaptation to imprisonment, including behaviour of incarcerated individuals, has been explained using two complementary perspectives: importation and deprivation theory. Deprivation theory focuses on characteristics of incarceration as determinants of prisoner adaption, and is often linked to the pains of imprisonment described by Sykes (1958). Later studies found that various prison and regime characteristics, including security level, opportunities for programming and recreation, and crowding, can be used to explain differences in offending (Baggio et al., 2020; Clark & Rydberg, 2016; Gaes & Camp, 2009; Lahm, 2009; Pompoco et al., 2017; Tahamont, 2019), and thus logically also victimisation.

Risks of both offending and victimisation may increase as the environment becomes more hostile or fails to offer meaningful activities to keep incarcerated individuals occupied. Importation theory holds that behaviour is largely a product of pre-existing values, traits, experiences and ideologies of individuals before entering prison (Irwin & Cressey, 1962). In relation to offending and victimisation, the theory suggests that incarcerated individuals are predisposed to behave in certain ways during incarceration, which shapes their risks of becoming offender or victim. Relevant 'imported' predictors of in-prison offending are age, race, gang affiliation, marital and parental status, offence and incarceration history and substance abuse history (DeLisi et al., 2011; Jiang & Fisher-Giorlando, 2002; Steiner et al., 2014; Walters & Crawford, 2013). Victimisation vulnerability, on the other hand, has been linked to age, race, education level, offence and incarceration history and mental illness, among other risk factors (Kuo, 2019; Lahm, 2015; Listwan et al.,

Table 1 Explanations for the victim-offender overlap in prisons

	Are victimisation and offending related?	Do victimisation and offending take place at the same time?	Are the roles clear and identifiable?	Situational or organised?
1: Mutual assault/fight	Yes: same incident	Yes: same incident	No: ambiguous	Situational
2: Retaliation	Yes: different but related incidents	No: different incidents	Yes: role reversal	Situational
3: Unrelated acts	No: different and unrelated incidents	No: different and unrelated incidents	Yes	Can vary for each incident
4: Illicit economy (contraband trade)	Yes: in the same incident or in different but related incidents	Yes and no: different roles in the same incidents, or different roles in different but related incidents	No, unless full information is available	Organised

2014; Steiner et al., 2017). In reference to Table 1, the shared importation and deprivation characteristics for victimisation and offending in prison accounts for the existence of a victim-offender overlap; however, the theories fall short in clarifying whether acts are related or unrelated, and situational or organised in nature.

Social control and opportunity theory (a theoretical perspective combining control and routine-activity theories) adds an important situational component to the deprivation and importation perspective: regardless of the strains of incarceration and individual risk factors, incidents are more likely to take place in the absence of guardianship (Choi & Wentling, 2021; Jiang & Fisher-Giorlando, 2002; McNeeley, 2021, 2022; Reyns et al., 2018; Steiner & Wooldredge, 2020). This means that unsupervised activities likely increase the risk of incidents, and make it more difficult to establish accurate accounts of what happened. Conversely, camera supervision at the very least can help identify offenders and victims, and disentangle the victim-offender overlap. Social control and opportunity theory can also account for the fact that people who engage in illicit activities in prison, for example using drugs, are more likely to become victims and offenders. In this sense, drug use and other activities associated with the illicit economy are part of a risky lifestyle, which increases exposure to risky situations and contributes to an individual's vulnerability to exploitation, extortion and (violent) debt recovery (Table 1, explanation 4). Through consideration of victim antagonism, social control and opportunity theory incorporates the mechanism of victim precipitation, which refers to the notion that victims may contribute to criminal events by creating circumstances that lead to victimisation or by provoking an aggressor (Table 1, explanation 1).[1]

Prior studies show that approximately 7% of incarcerated individuals in the US report that they committed physical or property offences and were also victimised (Daquin & Daigle, 2021; Toman, 2019). In the Netherlands, we have found similar numbers: in the Life in Custody Study, 6% of surveyed individuals self-reported victimisation and offending in the two months prior to the survey (Martens et al., 2021). We also compared characteristics of offenders, victims and victim-offenders, and found: (1) younger individuals more often report offending, but not victimisation; (2) individuals convicted of property offences report more offending and victimisation; (3) individuals in minimum-security regimes report victimisation and offending least often, while those in persistent-offender units report most offending. From these numbers we cannot deduce, however, whether there is a direct relationship between instances of offending and victimisation, or if the incidents are unrelated.

---

[1] This idea was first empirically tested by Wolfgang (1958), who found that 26% of homicide cases in Philadelphia in 1948-1952 could be classified as victim precipitated. The idea was later applied to other types of crimes, but heavily criticised for its victim-blaming implications and diverting attention away from systemic causes of crime (Timmer & Norman, 1984).

Research into the victim-offender overlap encounters multiple problems: first, the reasons for the overlap can vary widely, and the mechanisms for assaults and contraband-related incidents are likely different. Second, informing on fellow incarcerated individuals is considered 'snitching' or 'grassing' by the inmate code (Mitchell et al., 2017), and therefore official reports are unlikely to reflect the full truth that would be needed to establish roles and incident linkage. Researchers therefore have to collect their own data, which suffers from other limitations, not least of it the cost and effort of a sizeable project. Third, survey research thus far has been able to demonstrate that a victim-offender overlap exists, but not to what extent the aforementioned explanations can account for it. Interviews are arguably the best suitable method to connect separate incidents and triangulate accounts.

Two large-scale research projects in England and Wales have made especially important contributions to our understanding of the dynamics of the victim-offender overlap. In the first study, Edgar and O'Donnell (1998) surveyed and interviewed incarcerated individuals in two adult prisons and two young offender institutions on violent incidents (see also Edgar et al., 2003). They showed that various types of risky behaviour—including verbal or physical abuse of others and drug trading—can increase the risk of victimisation. One of the mechanisms behind the victim-offender overlap was victim precipitation, whereby the person who sustained the most serious injury had initiated the use of physical force (Table 1, explanation 1). Edgar and O'Donnell (1998) also illustrate how incarcerated individuals may engage in fights and commit assaults to reduce their perceived vulnerability and risk of victimisation. In many cases it may be difficult to determine who is victim or aggressor, particularly when this carries implications of blame: the contribution and role of parties may vary in terms of injury, who attacked first, and whose role or response could be considered more justifiable.

The second study, by Gooch and Treadwell (2020, 2022), offers insight in the victim-offender overlap in relation to the illicit economy (Table 1, explanation 4). They conducted ethnographic research on prison violence in three adult prisons and one young offender institution. Their research reveals a hierarchy of roles in relation to the trading of drugs, primarily spice[2] in prison. The businessmen are at the top of the hierarchy; they control the trading and make the most profit, and they do not usually use drugs themselves. They can become involved in physical conflicts—sometimes even with fatal endings—over the control of the drug trading business. Most businessmen are respected and liked by staff members, and they have extra privileges in prison as a result of their ostensibly good behaviour. The men who make up the middle layer of the hierarchy, the middle men and foot soldiers, do the leg work for a small margin of the profits. Their work consists of collecting, keeping and distributing the drugs in prison. They also do the accounting: managing payments and collecting debts, which can involve threats and physical aggression. Foot soldiers are sometimes made to fulfil this role under threat or coercion, which makes them both a victim and an offender. At the bottom of the hierarchy are the drug users. Drug use is considered an offence, but it also increases the risk of victimisation.

Drug use makes people vulnerable to victimisation through the accrual of debts and the reduced likelihood that they will report victimisation, given their own role in the economy. People may also be vulnerable because they have an intellectual disability or are susceptible to social pressure for other reasons. These individuals may be easily coerced into bringing drugs into prison, for example through visits or letters, hiding the drugs in their cell, or giving up drugs they brought in to more powerful others. Related to this, scholars have recognised forced drug searches as a special category of sexual assault (Banbury et al., 2016; Wilkinson & Fleming, 2021; Wilkinson, this volume). Such drug searches can include forcible stripping, visual genital inspection, intimate touching and internal intimate searches. Wilkinson and Fleming (2021) found that, in a ten-year period, 136 reported incidents could be identified as prisoner-on-prisoner drug searches in prisons in England and Wales (which is likely an underestimate). Compared to other types

---

[2] Spice is a synthetic drug that can be smoked. It is more difficult to detect than other drugs, because it has no odour and is invisible. It can be smuggled inside on drawings from children, fabricated legal letters, tax letters, and in clothes. It has a similar effect to THC in marihuana, but it is nearly impossible for users to know its strength. As a result, it is much more unpredictable and dangerous. Even small amounts of spice on paper have a large monetary value in prison.

of sexual assaults, drug searches were more likely to involve multiple perpetrators.

Of note are the changes that have taken place in the prison estate in England and Wales in the period between these two studies: while Edgar et al. (2003)—in their discussion of the victim-offender overlap—focus primarily on the dynamics of mutual assaults (Table 1, explanation 1) and retaliation (Table 1, explanation 2), Gooch and Treadwell (2020, 2022) emphasise the pervasive influence of the illicit economy (Table 1, explanation 4). This increased prominence of the illicit economy may be explained by various reasons, including physical deterioration of prison conditions, increases in the prison population coupled with staff shortages and technological developments (in particular, mobile phones and drone technology). As Gooch (2022) discusses, this also has theoretical implications: a culture of inmate solidarity and trading goods to ameliorate the pains of imprisonment as described by Sykes (1958) is largely superseded by a more professionalised illicit economy in which people take advantage of each other for individual gain and material survival. More generally, theories on offending and victimisation in prison should be revisited to (better) account for the victim-offender overlap.

This chapter adds a managerial perspective to the victim-offender overlap, particularly in relation to victimisation and offending in relation to the illicit prison economy (Table 1, explanation 4). The issues discussed above in relation to victimisation and offending are highly relevant to safety and order in prisons, and should therefore be a primary concern for prison managers. It may be difficult to effectively address the problem, however, if it is unclear who is victimised and who is responsible for the organisation of the illicit economy in prison. Gooch and Treadwell (2020) argued that the (changed) prison conditions particular to the Anglo-Welsh prison system are an important explanation for the changed nature of interpersonal dynamics, offending and victimisation and the omnipresence of illicit drugs (particularly spice) in the prisoner society. It is therefore informative to examine the extent to which these findings apply elsewhere, in this case to the Dutch prison system, and how prison managers approach the victim-offender overlap in terms of safety measures and sanctioning. The Dutch prison system, similar to the Anglo-Welsh system, has also dealt with budget cuts and an increased demand on incarcerated individuals' self-governance, which is reflected in cuts in programming and conditional access to certain privileges, such as extra visitation, more desirable jobs and early release. Unlike England and Wales, however, prisons in the Netherlands are not plagued by overcrowding, and most buildings date from 1996 and later, so the material conditions are generally better.

2 The Victim-Offender Overlap from a Prison-Management Perspective

As part of a research project on The Social Ecology of Violence in Prisons,[3] 45 prison managers (directors and deputy directors) were interviewed in 23 prisons in the Netherlands between January and June 2023.[4] This covers nearly the entire prison estate of the Netherlands, with the exception of one prison that opened during the research period. Prisons in the Netherlands can house individuals on remand and those who are convicted (in separate units). The average age of respondents was 54 (*range* = 38 – 67), 28 were men and 17 women. Interviews were conducted by the author of this chapter. They took place in a private office in the prison, respondents gave informed consent, and all interviews were recorded and transcribed verbatim.[5] Two interviews were conducted with two participants, other interviews were conducted one-to-one. On average, interviews lasted 70 minutes. Respondents were asked about the problems with violence and safety in their prison. The themes discussed in this chapter emerged inductively from the interviews and were analytically organised into the three challenges, which were checked against the data by repeated listening to and reading of the interviews. For the purpose of this chapter, a decision was made to focus on contraband trading (predominantly including cannabis and mobile phones), which was regarded by most prison managers as a large, if not

---

[3] This project is funded by the Dutch Research Council (NWO) as part of the research programme NWO Talent Programme Vidi (project number VI.vidi.211.003).
[4] Ethics approval was obtained for the study (Faculty of Law, Committee Ethics and Data, approval number 2022–040).
[5] Interviews were all held in Dutch. Quotes included in this chapter are translated from Dutch.

the largest, safety problem. They described a situation in which victimisation and offending are clearly overlapping, presenting special challenges for sanctioning. The findings discussed in this chapter apply primarily to the men's prisons; in women's prisons, contraband trading appeared less prevalent and less organised.[6]

2.1 Challenge 1: Prison Managers Are Required to Sanction Addiction-driven Drug Use

Drug use is prevalent in Dutch prisons. Prison managers report that cannabis is most often used, because it is—by far—most often identified in urine tests,[7] and also most often intercepted. It is also the most commonly used drug outside prison. Prison managers report feeling ambivalent about the drug use itself: the possession of small quantities of cannabis is condoned for private use in free society, and indeed, 23% of Dutch citizens reported ever having used cannabis, and 8% in the past year (Nationale Drug Monitor, 2022). Prison managers recognise that there are also recreative drug users among their staff. Pursuing the argument of normalisation, some prison managers would be open to considering how drug use can be regulated in prisons.

> In society, it has become normal, really, that you smoke a joint; you can buy it on the street corner. And inside, it is like it was twenty, thirty years back, it is simply not allowed. It is not tolerated, period. So yes, society has developed and prisons have stalled in this regard. (…) I think the transition is very large for some people. (Prison manager 2)
>
> Possession and use of soft drugs; we are busy hunting it down, while I am thinking, if you look at society and you want to normalise [imprisonment], soft drugs are used a lot. If you look at young people, it is really incredible, it is almost odd if you don't use. And here, we're are hunting it

---

[6] A detailed examination of this difference is beyond the scope of this chapter, but this was possibly related to the difference in criminal history of incarcerated women (i.e. they were less often involved in drug markets outside prison as leaders or dealers).
[7] Periodic urine tests are better able to identify cannabis use than use of other drugs, because cannabis leaves traces for longer.

down, while when someone has control over their use of soft drugs, you barely notice it. And it is sanctioned quite severely. I struggle with that sometimes, I think, yes, I am actually more worried about whether you are able to re-integrate properly and are in control of your drug use, than that I sanction you every time but nothing else. (Prison manager 21)

Yet, prison managers do not currently perceive alternatives to sanctioning. In line with current penitentiary policy, users who are caught typically receive a sanction of a few days cellular confinement without television.[8] This concern with re-integration noted by Prison manager 21, is also iterated by other interviewees. The current approach of sanctioning drug use does not equip people with skills to manage their drug use responsibly, or deal with the issues that are related to their drug use.

If you want to teach people to deal with their problems and you keep them away from those problems, then you can't teach them. (…) With soft drugs [e.g. cannabis], this is so accepted in society, while here you keep them away from it, while on the outside it often has a relation to the problems of why they are in here. So, if you want to teach them to deal with that, it is a bit strange to keep them away from it. At the same time, I understand the political sensitivity and everything around it, but I think it is something that you should at least discuss, instead of rigidly saying, "no, drugs are never allowed in prison." (Prison manager 23)

This current rigid approach is underscored by the additional consequence that detected drug use leads to the mandatory removal of privileges (i.e. demotion to the basic programme) for at least six weeks if they were in the plus programme; this programme entitles people to an additional hour of visitation, private visits, more time out of cell, and is a requirement for some jobs or training and conditional release eligibility. Prison managers struggle especially with this second consequence, because demotion to the basic programme is regarded as interfering with re-integration preparation for people who may need it the most. Furthermore, they consider it double punishment for people who have

---

[8] A distinction is made between 'soft drugs' including cannabis, magic mushrooms and benzodiazepines, and 'hard drugs' including cocaine, ecstasy, heroin and GHB. Spice is sanctioned in prison as a hard drug. Hard drugs are sanctioned more severely.

a limited ability to control their drug use because they are addicted and exposed to opportunities to buy and use drugs in prison. Respondents are worried that demotion discourages drug users from trying to address their addiction and other (often related) problems.

> I may have someone who wants to stop using [cannabis], has been clean for two years, I am just making up an example, has a smoke from a joint on the yard, and I need to demote them straight away. If something is stupid, it's that. "Well, if this is how it goes, then I'll just start smoking cannabis again." (Prison manager 1)

> I was raised with the idea that if you are addicted, you are ill. That has been researched quite a lot. Now it's the case that someone who is addicted and uses drugs here, I should punish for their illness. And on the one hand, I always punish, a disciplinary sanction, cellular confinement without television, but I also need to demote someone right away. And with that I think, well, that's someone with an illness, really, who you are giving pretty much a double punishment, while that's very different from someone who decidedly says, "it was my birthday, I wanted a joint, I smoked a joint." I really think that's different. (Prison manager 4)

These examples illustrate that mandatory demotion fails to recognise the difficult reality of substance recovery, and can have the opposite effect from what is intended. The interviews also reveal that treatment is not considered a very accessible alternative to a sanction in regular prison and pre-trial units (specialised units with more direct involved of psychologists appear to have more treatment options).

Prison managers also report that the use of cannabis does not ostensibly lead to more problem behaviour by the drug users and does not directly threaten safety.

> With soft drugs, it is not generally the case that people become very aggressive. Soft drugs are calming, so it doesn't directly affect safety. (…) The possession and use [of soft drugs] itself never leads to many problems. (Prison manager 38)

In fact, the absence of problems and the presence of a more peaceful atmosphere are even seen as indicators that are drugs inside.

> When it's really relaxed [the atmosphere], there usually is also a lot [drugs]. Then it's peaceful. And then we know something, we catch something, and hoppa [things are not peaceful anymore]. So in a way you can say we create our own problem. (Prison manager 2)

> There are weeks we don't have anything inside and then we are very satisfied. [The national search unit] will come and they will find absolutely nothing. That means we're completely clean, but you also see in the behaviour that there is a lot of unrest. (Prison manager 39)

The problems and unrest referred to by these prison managers can entail fights because drugs are intercepted and scores are settled regarding perceptions of blame or debts, or because people try to find ways to acquire drugs again. The no-drugs policy is at odds with society outside, but its enforcement is also a constant and—to some extent—unsuccessful battle. Certainly not every prison manager would support the idea of regulating drug use, but the current situation is recognised by most as unsatisfactory.

> People are addicted. Do we not handle this too punitively? That is more a moral dilemma I, myself, have. When I think what starts trouble here it's drugs, because they want to get their hands on it. That gives conflict, because if it goes wrong with the import, debts will be settled, because they still have to pay. That's why it's the biggest problem. (Prison manager 39)

The fact that soft drugs are not distributed in any legal or medical fashion creates a market for illegal trading, which in turn creates problems of exploitation and violence. While more treatment options are considered desirable, the majority of prisoners do not serve long sentences, so their stay is too short to treat their addiction problems adequately:

> The average time someone spends here is between 15 and 75 days. I do not have the illusions that I will turn them into model citizens. (Prison manager 39)

Some prison managers also express an understanding for the use of drugs to decrease stress levels and relax, especially considering the difficult circumstances that often surround imprisonment and the lack of distractions when people are behind their door. It is seen as a problem that easy access to drugs may interfere with addiction recovery, and even encourages people who have never used drugs to start using. This is a valid concern considering that a recent Belgian study reported that 14% of surveyed individuals reported that they started using drugs in prison (Favril, 2023). The largest problem related to drug use is—the same as in free society—that it requires the supply of drugs, which is associated with far-stretching and highly profitable criminal activities. There are various tasks in the supply chain of contraband, particularly the distribution of drugs, where the roles of victim and offender are ambiguous or difficult to prove. Unregulated drug use, addiction and associated debt accrual make people vulnerable to exploitation in the supply chain.

2.2 Challenge 2: Prison Manager Often Sanction People Who Act Under Duress

Prison managers suspect that many contraband-related offences are committed under duress. Typical offences that are done by 'foot soldiers' (Gooch & Treadwell, 2020) are hiding contraband in one's cell, receiving drugs during a visit (sometimes with unknown visitors), collecting contraband thrown over the wall or dropped by a drone or returning with drugs after temporary release.

> Prisoners sometimes tell me "I am pressured", but they often won't say by whom, because they don't want to inform on each other. But I get a lot of information when I talk to them for sanctioning purposes. When I ask, "what really happened?" Well, eventually-, you know, often they first say nothing, but when you keep asking you find out that conflicts are often about drugs, or use, or things they promised each other, or people

are put under pressure to bring things in, you know, when they go on temporary release. So I think drug use itself, if someone smokes a joint in the evening on their cell-, well, it's not good of course, but I think the indirect effects are really worrisome. (Prison manager 26)

The indirect effects this prison manager refers to are the dynamics of the drug trade, which means that these people commit offences but are also victimised by others: they are put under pressure using threats, or because they feel powerless to refuse demands by others. For example, when contraband is found in a double cell, both residents are held responsible, unless one person is evidently blameless. Prison managers suspect that it is not uncommon that the person who admits to hiding contraband in a cell is covering for their cellmate. They often sanction the person who confessed, even knowing that they are likely not the true offender. When prison managers suspect this or when a person admits they committed the offence under duress, a sanction is still perceived as the only option, unless a person gives information on whose orders they were acting (which they usually refuse to do).

> When you're talking about violence and aggression, some guys have nothing to lose, so that makes it easier for them to take a risk, let themselves be used, or they think it's fine. (…)
>
> *Interviewer: Is it always clear for you who is the victim or who is the offender, when you have to sanction people?*
>
> Not always. But you notice-, staff often do know this and will say, "yes, he is confessing now, but we know for sure, [his cellmate] is clearly the dominant of the two." (…) And when they confess, I'll sometimes say to them, "then I can do nothing but give you a punishment." But I'll sometimes, when I talk to them in segregation, say to them, "are you sure?" (…) "I have a feeling that you are taking the blame for this other person." I'll try to tell them and staff do as well, but it's up to them to make the choice. (Prison manager 12)

People at all levels in the chain of drug use and distribution will hesitate to trust staff members about incidents of victimisation for various reasons. Because everyone in this chain fulfils an illegal role—making everyone an offender—it is extremely difficult to unearth what has happened and who is responsible. Moreover, informing on others—if discovered—usually also leads to victimisation. This also means that staff need to act very carefully if they suspect that people are coerced into bringing drugs into prison or hiding them in their cell: if they transfer someone to another wing, this can raise suspicions that someone has talked, which can endanger this person. The line between victimisation and offending is very thin in these cases. Even though it is difficult to elicit information from prisoners, there are other ways for staff to draw inferences about offending and victimisation. Prison managers report the following as signs of possible victimisation or fear of victimisation related to the illicit economy: inexplicable injuries (i.e. injuries that appear the result of assault but that a person does not want to explain), withdrawal from life on the unit (self-isolation), and requests to be transferred to another unit or prison. People with an intellectual disability are considered especially vulnerable to exploitation; an estimated 45% of people in Dutch prisons fall in this category (Kaal, 2016). The size of this group also means that the problem is considered difficult to manage: in cases of proven victimisation people may be transferred to other units or prisons for their own protection, but without evidence transfers are often not possible. Prevention of victimisation is difficult, partly because those who are responsible often remain under the radar.

2.3 Challenge 3: The Leaders 'In Charge' of the Illicit Economy Are Difficult to Sanction

The illegal activities of the leaders (the 'business men' in Gooch & Treadwell, 2020) are less visible, because they use other people to receive and distribute drugs. Their illegal activities are much more circumspect, and usually involve communication with sources outside prison. These leaders tend to be imprisoned for more serious crimes and therefore have lengthy sentences, which often comes with respect and status among peers. Their lengthy prison stay gives them time to build a network and business inside prison, and gain privileges. It also makes it more difficult for frontline staff to set clear limits on their behaviour; staff often build a relationship with incarcerated individuals on their unit over time, and a certain give-and-take is common to make their work easier. Examples may be the provision of an extra mattress, accepting cell inventories not wholly in line with requirements, or allowing time out of cell beyond what is formally allowed. It is more difficult for staff to renege these privileges after having condoned them for a while. While good staff-prisoner relationships are associated with a safe prison climate, too much laxity in the enforcement of rules can also create conditions for illicit activities. The uncovering of the contribution of leaders to these activities requires time, resources and attentive staff.

There are various methods that can reveal who fulfils a leadership position in the illicit economy. All Dutch prisons have a Bureau of Intelligence and Security that can trace money transfers between prison accounts, and can also listen in to phone conversations (people need to be notified of this). Staff can help identify leaders by paying attention to (and mapping) social relations on a unit: who are the people often surrounded by others, who are given preferential treatment, for example access to phones, who make decisions about recreational activities such as gaming and watching television, and who do not get involved in conflicts but can often be found watching from a distance? Other identifiers are the way luxury and canteen items appear to be distributed among people in the unit: giving away items can be seen as a way to win over more vulnerable individuals and create a feeling of indebtedness and gratitude.

> When certain people come in, with familiar names, you immediately see people swarming around them, giving them canteen products for free, so then you know already, those are the foot soldiers who will be doing all sorts of things. We keep a sharp eye on that, and we write about it in the reports. It's signalling and reporting, but very difficult to get a good grip on what is going on. Because they [the leaders] stay right under the surface, so that they aren't visible. (Prison manager 8)

Their leadership is not visible through bad behaviour, but instead can be identified—paradoxically—because they behave ostensibly well, and are usually (exceptionally) polite to staff. It is in their best interest to avoid unrest, such as cell inspections, because this disrupts their business. They may have jobs with more privileges, such as a cleaning job, which allows them to conduct business more freely. Any of the aforementioned identifiers are hardly punishable, and this type of profiling also carries a risk of false accusations and the imposition of unfair or unwarranted restrictions. This makes reporting this behaviour more difficult, and sanctioning even more so. Sometimes, suspicious behaviour may be revealed through extensive investigations, for example money transfers.

> Then we looked into the information behind the scenes, so not what we observe but information we have, and he turned out to be the City Bank. (…) We identified many financial transactions all leading to him. So yes, he had an interest in appearing as friendly as possible so he could manage his business. So you see some things on the front stage that are visible, but we also pay attention to the back stage. (Prison manager 11)

In this particular case, the money transfers were not illegal and thus not punishable, but it was decided not to extend the person's job contract as cleaner, in which he was able to move freely around the prison. Alternatively, prison managers—when they have received multiple signals that someone may be in charge of illicit activities and use others to do work for them—try to disrupt the relations by moving the person to another unit. The effects of such measures on victimisation and offending have not yet been studied, but certainly deserve attention.

3 Conclusion

The picture emerging from interviews with Dutch prison managers shows that contraband trading is one of the largest safety problems they are currently facing, and that this is responsible for complex dynamics related to victimisation and offending. The explanations for involvement in the illicit prison economy (and related victimisation and offending) vary depending on one's role. Deprivation and importation factors are still highly relevant for the drug users. They create the demand, because they want to use drugs to pass the time and enjoy its effects, or because they are addicted and cannot control their use. In response to this demand, the contraband trade has become professionalised, involves large sums of money and is tied to criminal activity and networks outside prison. Deprivation theory is not as relevant an explanation for the leaders in charge; those at the top of the pyramid stand to gain much more than just a compensation for lacking services and goods in prison; contraband trading is a lucrative business model with gains inside and outside prison. Their role is often a continuation of criminal activity from outside prison; and indeed, many of the same dynamics can be witnessed in relation to drug trading and organised crime outside prison. Similar to dynamics of these crimes outside prison (Jacobs, 2000; Jacobs & Wright, 2006), involvement in the trade (particularly as a user or merchant, who receives, keeps or distributes goods) creates a risky lifestyle, which makes people vulnerable to victimisation if debts are not settled or anything goes awry, such as an intercepted delivery. Additionally, they are vulnerable to victimisation because their own criminal involvement reduces the likelihood that they will report anything. Finally, cultural norms obscure who fulfils what role, because informing on others is considered unacceptable. In the current study it became clear that even when prison managers would receive information, they were often unable to act directly on it, because they did not have hard evidence, and they had to consider the safety (but also possible ulterior motives, such as framing someone) of the person who reported the information.

The three challenges discussed in this chapter reveal the difficulties of addressing victimisation and offending—particularly in relation to the drug economy in prison—fairly and effectively. Prison managers struggle with balancing policy directives, re-integration needs, concerns for an individual's safety and safety and order in the prison more generally. Various recommendations may be considered for reducing offending and victimisation related to the drug economy. First, drug trading would not be so lucrative without so many drug users. While treatment is no panacea for resolving this problem, more treatment options—also in regular units—would be a worthwhile alternative or addition to sanctioning. In particular, it should be considered whether people who accept treatment for substance use can retain their privileges in the plus programme. Drug use may also lose some of its attraction if more activities are offered to occupy one's mind and time, also on evenings and weekend days. Second, it should be explored whether treatment and education programmes could be combined with regulated distribution of cannabis, again with the aim to discourage trading, as well as to monitor the use of drugs and prevent the use of more harmful substances, including spice. It would be strongly advisable to evaluate such a harm reduction policy with a randomised controlled trial.[9] In general, considering the prevalence of drug use among the incarcerated population, it would be pertinent to consider how people can manage their drug use while simultaneously working on their re-integration. Third, staff supervision is important for preventing opportunities for offending and victimisation. While the staff-to-prisoner ratio contributes to staff's ability to observe and intervene in offending, other factors such as lay-out and visibility are equally important. Small units with a central staff office and good visibility of the entire unit, including the living/recreation room, reduce opportunities for illicit activities. Finally, prison managers were strongly in favour of installing in-cell telephones to increase legitimate opportunities to call loved ones and reduce the need for obtaining illegal phones. This would also help distinguish more clearly between people using a phone for continued criminal activity, versus those who use it for less nefarious purposes.[10]

The picture emerging from the interviews with Dutch prison managers shows important similarities and differences with prior research, in particular the research conducted by Gooch and Treadwell. A striking similarity is the prevalence of drugs in prison, and the professionalised nature of the trade. The sharpest difference with England and Wales is that the use and trade of spice do not appear to be nearly as prominent. In the Netherlands, cannabis was identified as the primary

---

[9] The use of cannabis is not risk-free, especially for people with a predisposition for psychotic illnesses. An evaluation study should therefore also consider whether the use among people in this group decreases as a result of the proposed intervention.

[10] In-cell telephones were installed in some prisons in the Netherlands, and prison managers reported positive experiences. In addition to reducing the demand for illegal phones (which is yet to be examined quantitatively), it reportedly caused less unrest when evening programmes had to be cancelled, and removed conflict about the use of public phones on the wing.

drug of choice. The health and behavioural risks associated with the use of cannabis are, arguably, less serious than with the use of spice. This was in line with the nature and seriousness of incidents described in the interviews (i.e. less serious than described by Gooch & Treadwell, 2020, and little to no evidence of drug-related sexual assaults as described by Wilkinson & Fleming, 2021).[11] The apparent difference in seriousness of incidents between England and Wales and the Netherlands may have various explanations. First, cannabis as the preferred choice of drugs arguably carries less risk; this preference may be explained by the fact that spice has a much smaller presence in the Netherlands in general, while cannabis is very easily acquired and normalised to some extent. Second, the prison conditions in the Netherlands do not appear nearly as dire as in England and Wales, staff experience, presence and control appear greater and prison managers were actively trying to disrupt harmful power relations, and had some resources to investigate beyond immediately visible behaviour. At the same time, there were signals that staff shortages in some prisons threatened (perceived) safety, and led to reduced daily programmes which may in turn increase the attractiveness of drug use and continued criminal activity while people are locked up. The picture painted in studies conducted in England and Wales should be taken as a warning sign: an under-resourced prison system fails at even its most basic function of incapacitation, which carries severe health and safety risks for its population of incarcerated individuals and, ultimately, wider society.

---

[11] Prison managers were explicitly asked about their awareness of sexual assaults, but this was very rarely reported. Contrary to the situation in England and Wales, Dutch prison managers were not familiar with the phenomenon of drug-related sexual assaults.

References

Baggio, S., Peigné, N., Heller, P., Gétaz, L., Liebrenz, M., & Wolff, H. (2020). Do overcrowding and turnover cause violence in prison? *Frontiers in Psychiatry, 10*, 1015–1019. https://doi.org/10.3389/fpsyt.2019.01015

Banbury, S., Lusher, J., & Morgan, W. (2016). Male sexual aggressors in the British prison service: An exploratory study. *International Journal of Mental Health and Addiction, 14*(4), 370–384. https://doi.org/10.1007/s11469-016-9678-y

Beijersbergen, K. A., Dirkzwager, A. J. E., Eichelsheim, V. I., Van der Laan, P. H., & Nieuwbeerta, P. (2015). Procedural justice, anger, and prisoners' misconduct. *Criminal Justice and Behavior, 42*, 196–218. https://doi.org/10.1177/0093854814550710

Berghuis, M. L., Sentse, M., Palmen, H., & Nieuwbeerta, P. (2021). Receiving visits in prison and aggressive and contraband misconduct among Dutch prisoners. *European Journal of Criminology, 20*(4), 1369–1389. https://doi.org/10.1177/14773708211041016

Bosma, A. Q., Van Ginneken, E. F. J. C., Sentse, M., & Palmen, H. (2020). Examining prisoner misconduct: A multilevel test using personal characteristics, prison climate, and prison environment. *Crime & Delinquency, 66*, 451–484. https://doi.org/10.1177/0011128719877347

Camp, S. D., Gaes, G. G., Langan, N. P., & Saylor, W. G. (2003). The influence of prisons on inmate misconduct: A multilevel investigation. *Justice Quarterly, 20*, 501–533. https://doi.org/10.1080/07418820300095601

Caravaca-Sánchez, F., & Wolff, N. (2017). The association between substance use and physical victimization among incarcerated men in Spanish prisons. *Law and Psychiatry, 50*, 9–16. https://doi.org/10.1016/j.ijlp.2016.09.006

Caravaca-Sánchez, F., Wolff, N., & Teasdale, B. (2019). Exploring associations between interpersonal violence and prison size in Spanish prisons. *Crime & Delinquency, 65*, 2019–2043. https://doi.org/10.1177/0011128718763134

Choi, J., & Wentling, R. (2021). Convict code, risky lifestyles, and violent victimization among inmates in South Korea. *Violence and Victims, 36*(2), 233–250. https://doi.org/10.1891/VV-D-19-00118

Clark, K., & Rydberg, J. (2016). The effect of institutional educational programming on prisoner misconduct. *Criminal Justice Studies, 29*(4), 325–344. https://doi.org/10.1080/1478601X.2016.1229770

Daquin, J., & Daigle, L. (2021). The victim–offender overlap in prison: Examining the factors associated with group membership. *Journal of Interpersonal*

Violence, 36(23–24), NP13439 –NP13462. https://doi.org/10.1177/088 6260519898427

DeLisi, M., Trulson, C. R., Marquart, J. W., Drury, A. J., & Kosloski, A. E. (2011). Inside the prison black box: Toward a life course importation model of inmate behavior. *International Journal of Offender Therapy and Comparative Criminology, 55*(8), 1186–1207. https://doi.org/10.1177/0306624X1 1383956

Drury, A. J., & DeLisi, M. (2010). The past is prologue: Prior adjustment to prison and institutional misconduct. *The Prison Journal, 90*, 331–352. https://doi.org/10.1177/0032885510375676

Edgar, K., & O'Donnell, I. (1998). Assault in prison: The 'victim's' contribution. *The British Journal of Criminology, 38*(4), 635–650. http://www.jstor.org/stable/23638743

Edgar, K., O'Donnell, I., & Martin, C. (2003). *Prison violence: The dynamics of conflict, fear and power*. Willan Publishing.

Favril, L. (2023). Drug use before and during imprisonment: Drivers of continuation. *International Journal of Drug Policy, 115*, 1–7. https://doi.org/10.1016/j.drugpo.2023.104027

Gaes, G. G., & Camp, S. D. (2009). Unintended consequences: Experimental evidence for the criminogenic effect of prison security level placement on post-release recidivism. *Journal of Experimental Criminology, 5*(2), 139–162. https://doi.org/10.1007/s11292-009-9070-z

Gaes, G. G., Wallace, S., Gilman, E., Klein-Saffran, J., & Suppa, S. (2002). The influence of prison gang affiliation on violence and other prison misconduct. *The Prison Journal, 82*(3), 359–385. https://doi.org/10.1177/003288 550208200304

Gooch, K. (2022). "Just don't wear prison issue!": Material deprivation, material machismo, and the illicit prison economy. In B. Crewe, A. Goldsmith, & M. Halsey (Eds.), *Power and pain in the modern prison: The society of captives revisited* (pp. 193-C110.P158). Oxford University Press. https://doi.org/10.1093/oso/9780198859338.003.0011

Gooch, K., & Treadwell, J. (2020). Prisoner society in an era of psychoactive substances, organized crime, new drug markets and austerity. *The British Journal of Criminology, 60*(5), 1260–1281. https://doi.org/10.1093/bjc/aza a019

Gooch, K., & Treadwell, J. (2022). The 'screw boys' and the 'businessmen': Re-Negotiating penal power, governance and legitimate authority through a prison violence reduction scheme. *The British Journal of Criminology, 63*, 1219–1236. https://doi.org/10.1093/bjc/azac081

Goossens, E., Robert, L., & Daems, T. (2023). Individual and contextual risk factors of prisoners' victimization: A best fit framework synthesis. *Aggression and Violent Behavior, 70*, 1–16. https://doi.org/10.1016/j.avb.2023.101826

Irwin, J., & Cressey, D. (1962). Thieves, convicts and the inmate culture. *Social Problems, 10*, 142–155.

Jacobs, B. A. (2000). *Robbing drug dealers: Violence beyond the law*. Routledge.

Jacobs, B. A., & Wright, R. (2006). *Street justice: Retaliation in the criminal underworld*. Cambridge University Press.

Jiang, S., & Fisher-Giorlando, M. (2002). Inmate misconduct: A test of the deprivation, importation, and situational models. *The Prison Journal, 82*, 335–358. https://doi.org/10.1177/003288550208200303

Kaal, H. (2016). *Prevalentie licht verstandelijke beperking in het justitiedomein*. Hogeschool Leiden.

Kuo, S.-Y., Chang, K.-M., Chen, Y.-S., Lai, Y.-L., Chang, Y.-S., & Li, Y. (2022). Assessing the victim–offender overlap in prison victimization and misconduct among Taiwanese male inmates. *The British Journal of Criminology, 62*(3), 585–606. https://doi.org/10.1093/bjc/azab066

Kuo, S. (2019). Prison Victimization among Taiwanese male inmates: An application of importation, deprivation, and routine activities theories. *Security Journal, 33*(4), 602–621. https://doi.org/10.1057/s41284-019-00202-9

Lahm, K. (2016). Official incidents of inmate-on-inmate misconduct at a women's prison: Using importation and deprivation theories to compare perpetrators to victims. *Criminal Justice Studies, 29*(3), 214–231. https://doi.org/10.1080/1478601X.2016.1154263

Lahm, K. F. (2009). Educational participation and inmate misconduct. *Journal of Offender Rehabilitation, 48*(1), 37–52. https://doi.org/10.1080/10509670802572235

Lahm, K. F. (2015). Predictors of violent and nonviolent victimization behind bars: An exploration of women inmates. *Women & Criminal Justice, 25*(4), 273–291. https://doi.org/10.1080/08974454.2014.989304

Listwan, S. J., Daigle, L. E., Hartman, J. L., & Guastaferro, W. P. (2014). Poly-victimization risk in prison: The influence of individual and institutional factors. *Journal of Interpersonal Violence, 29*(13), 2458–2481. https://doi.org/10.1177/0886260513518435

Logan, M. W., Long, J., DeLisi, M., & Hazelwood, A. R. (2022). Serious, violent, and chronic prison misconduct: Are the predictors the same for women and men? *The Prison Journal, 103*(1), 23–44. https://doi.org/10.1177/00328855221139855

Martens, S., Van Ginneken, E. F. J. C., & Palmen, H. (2021). Slachtofferschap en slachtoffer-daderschap in Nederlandse penitentiaire inrichtingen. *Tijdschrift Voor Criminologie, 63*(4), 399–422. https://doi.org/10.5553/TvC/0165182X2021063004002

McNeeley, S. (2021). Situational Risk factors for inmate-on-staff assaults. *The Prison Journal, 10*(3), 352–373. https://doi.org/10.1177/00328855211010478

McNeeley, S. (2022). Reaffirming the relationship between routine activities and violent victimization in prison. *Journal of Criminal Justice, 78*, 101883. https://doi.org/10.1016/j.jcrimjus.2022.101883

Mitchell, M. M., Fahmy, C., Pyrooz, D. C., & Decker, S. H. (2017). Criminal Crews, codes, and contexts: Differences and similarities across the code of the street, convict code, street gangs, and prison gangs. *Deviant Behavior, 38*(10), 1197–1222. https://doi.org/10.1080/01639625.2016.1246028

Nationale Drug Monitor. (2022). *Nationale drug monitor: Kerncijfers en ontwikkelingen 2021 [National drug monitor: Core numbers and developments 2021]*. Trimbos-instituut & WODC.

Pérez, D. M., Gover, A. R., Tennyson, K. M., & Santos, S. D. (2010). Individual and institutional characteristics related to inmate victimization. *International Journal of Offender Therapy and Comparative Criminology, 54*, 378–394. https://doi.org/10.1177/0306624X09335244

Pompoco, A., Wooldredge, J., Lugo, M., Sullivan, C., & Latessa, E. J. (2017). Reducing inmate misconduct and prison returns with facility education programs. *Criminology & Public Policy, 16*(2), 515–547. https://doi.org/10.1111/1745-9133.12290

Reyns, B. W., Woo, Y., Lee, H. D., & Yoon, O.-K. (2018). Vulnerability versus opportunity: Dissecting the role of low self-control and risky lifestyles in violent victimization risk among Korean inmates. *Crime & Delinquency, 64*, 423–447. https://doi.org/10.1177/0011128716679375

Steiner, B., Butler, H. D., & Ellison, J. (2014). Causes and correlates of prison inmate misconduct: A systematic review of the evidence. *Journal of Criminal Justice, 42*(6), 462–470. https://doi.org/10.1016/j.jcrimjus.2014.08.001

Steiner, B., Ellison, J. M., Butler, H. D., & Cain, C. M. (2017). The impact of inmate and prison characteristics on prisoner victimization. *Trauma, Violence, & Abuse, 18*, 17–36. https://doi.org/10.1177/1524838015588503

Steiner, B., & Wooldredge, J. (2020). *Understanding and reducing prison violence: An integrated social control-opportunity perspective*. Routledge.

Sykes, G. (1958). *The society of captives: A study of a maximum security prison*. Princeton University Press.

Tahamont, S. (2019). The effect of facility security classification on serious rules violation reports in California prisons: A regression discontinuity design. *Journal of Quantitative Criminology, 35*(4), 767–796. https://doi.org/10.1007/s10940-019-09405-0

Timmer, D. A., & Norman, W. H. (1984). The ideology of victim precipitation. *Criminal Justice Review, 9*(2), 63–68. https://doi.org/10.1177/073401688400900209

Toman, E. L. (2019). The victim-offender overlap behind bars: Linking prison misconduct and victimization. *Justice Quarterly, 36*(2), 350–382. https://doi.org/10.1080/07418825.2017.1402072

Walters, G. D., & Crawford, G. (2013). In and out of prison: Do importation factors predict all forms of misconduct or just the more serious ones? *Journal of Criminal Justice, 41*(6), 407–413. https://doi.org/10.1016/j.jcrimjus.2013.08.001

Wilkinson, J., & Fleming, J. (2021). Prisoner-on-prisoner drug searches in prisons in England and Wales: 'Business as usual.' *Incarceration, 2*(2), 1–17. https://doi.org/10.1177/26326663211015852

Wolff, N., Shi, J., & Siegel, J. (2009). Understanding physical victimization inside prisons: Factors that predict risk. *Justice Quarterly, 26*, 445–475. https://doi.org/10.1080/07418820802427858

Wolfgang, M. (1958). *Patterns in criminal homicide*. University of Pennsylvania Press.

Vulnerability and Victimhood in Prison: Reflecting on the Concept of Vulnerability in Prisoner Victimisation Research

Aurore Vanliefde

Within this book on prisoner victimisation, this chapter provides a conceptual reflection on the concept of 'vulnerability' in the context of victimisation studies. As in several chapters in this book, prisoner victimisation studies often analyse specific characteristics in relation to victimisation experiences. The term 'vulnerable' is then used to highlight the increased risk of discrimination and victimisation of minority groups in prisoner victimisation research. As a result, victimological-penological scientific literature and human rights law tends to categorise specific groups of people as 'vulnerable' based on characteristics such as age, gender identity, disability, ethnicity, religion, sexual orientation or socio-economic situation. Some authors speak of a 'Vulnerability Turn' within law and social sciences, due to its extensive use (Burgorgue-Larsen, 2014; Le Blanc, 2019; Soulet, 2014a, 2014b). This chapter invites the reader to reflect on the term 'vulnerable' in prisoner victimisation research and promotes a considerate use of the concept. Issues related to the concept

---

A. Vanliefde (✉)
Faculty of Law and Criminology, KU Leuven, Leuven, Belgium
e-mail: aurore.vanliefde@kuleuven.be

© The Author(s), under exclusive license to Springer Nature Switzerland AG 2024
T. Daems and E. Goossens (eds.), *Understanding Prisoner Victimisation*, Palgrave Studies in Victims and Victimology, https://doi.org/10.1007/978-3-031-54350-0_5

of vulnerability have already been addressed in the fields of philosophy, human rights law and political science, but this reflection is of considerable importance for prisoner victimisation studies as well.

While the concept of vulnerability can serve as a valuable tool for recognising and addressing discrimination, victimisation experiences and specific needs, its use also carries inherent risks (including essentialism, stigmatisation and paternalism) that must be carefully navigated. This chapter's aim is to invite researchers, policymakers and practitioners to reflect on the implications of and the discursive power dynamics when using the concept of vulnerability in reference to incarcerated people. As prisoner victimisation studies can inform prison policy and practice, the author argues for a considerate and nuanced use of the concept of vulnerability. When focusing on vulnerability in relation to a specific context, the concept can be particularly valuable as to uncover institutional and structural power dynamics which contribute to this victimisation process, while recognising the individual differences and resilience of incarcerated persons considered as vulnerable.

As victimisation can take on many forms, looking at victimhood in prison through the lens of vulnerability is especially helpful to make institutional forms of discrimination and violence visible. Indeed, by failing to meet specific needs of minorities due to prison regimes and their infrastructure, these groups are significantly more discriminated against. However, the concept of vulnerability can also result in more harmful outcomes when used in an unnuanced or reductionist manner. Systematically categorising groups of people as vulnerable solely based on their identity characteristics can be essentialising and stigmatising. This stigmatisation is not only at risk of occurring in the discourse surrounding them but also in practice. For example, labelling certain groups of people as vulnerable can lead to specific protective measures, such as isolating people from the general prison population, increasing the visibility of these persons and limiting their access to activities, work and services. Additionally, 'vulnerability' can be experienced by minorities as being imposed on them, dismissing individual differences and the resilience of incarcerated persons facing victimisation. In those cases, the concept of vulnerability can inspire paternalistic interventions aimed at managing risks inherent to their perceived vulnerability and be instrumentalised to feed existing power dynamics within the institution of the prison.

This chapter begins with an outline of the concept of vulnerability and distinguishes the characteristic-based approach towards vulnerability from the context-based approach. Keeping these theoretical considerations in mind, the second part focuses on vulnerability and incarcerated persons. Finally, the main limitations to and concerns regarding the use of the concept of vulnerability are discussed in the last part of this chapter. More specifically, the risks of essentialism, stigmatisation and paternalism are considered and applied to prisoner victimisation.

1 A Closer Look at the Concept of Vulnerability

The emergence of the concept of vulnerability has been studied extensively in the field of human rights law, mainly by analysing its use in the jurisprudence of the European Court of Human Rights (ECtHR) (Carlier, 2017; Peroni & Timmer, 2013; Rota, 2020; Ruet, 2015; Timmer, 2013; Turner, 2006; Zimmermann, 2015, 2022). Since the early 2010s, several authors have denounced its vague and extending nature (Blondel, 2015; Brodiez-Dolino, 2014; Ruet, 2015). Where some state that 'vulnerability is everywhere' (Le Blanc, 2019), others qualify it a catch-all-concept (Brodiez-Dolino, 2014) or even a 'sponge word' (Faberon, 2014: 52) due to its intrinsic malleable nature, its capacity to gather a multitude of meanings and its lack of clear outline. Furthermore, human rights law researchers have argued that the overuse of the term carries the risk of it becoming void of any meaning (Clément & Buldoc, 2004; Zimmermann, 2022). This resonates with Stanley Cohen's (1989) critique of the concept of 'social control', of which he warned for the risk to become a 'hammering concept', used like a little boy pounding his toy hammer on everything he encounters.

Vulnerability has also been theorised in philosophy and ethics, most notably in relation to the ethics of care (Gilligan, 1982; Tronto, 1993, 2009), the relation to the self (Levinas, 1998) or as a universal aspect indissociable from human condition (amongst others, see Fineman,

2008, 2013; Mackenzie et al., 2014; Nussbaum, 2001, 2006). A reiteration of conducted work on the matter (see for example Blondel, 2015; Maillard, 2011; Zimmermann, 2022) falls outside of the scope of this contribution. The focus of this chapter is to understand vulnerability in the sense of identifying certain characteristics which make well-defined categories of people more 'vulnerable' to victimisation in prison with the aim of reflecting on the implications of this qualification.

In scientific literature, mainly in medicine and social sciences, 'vulnerability' is used to describe the state of being exposed to the possibility of being harmed (by a substance, by other living beings or by societal norms and institutions). In the specific context of prisoner victimisation, vulnerability is used to highlight the experiences and needs of groups who are more likely to be harmed in some way because of certain characteristics. However, regarding vulnerability as merely being the direct consequence of the presence of a certain characteristic does not suffice for understanding mechanisms which lie at the root of this vulnerability. Instead, placing vulnerability within the specific context in which it occurs can contribute to uncovering structural issues from which vulnerability originates. In what follows, both the characteristic-based and the context-based approach towards vulnerability are discussed further.

1.1 Characteristic-based Vulnerability

The characteristic-based approach to using the term 'vulnerability' is recurrent in scientific literature, but also in policy documents and human rights law. This often takes the form of a (non-exhaustive) list of categories of people with specific characteristics or objective criteria (Spiers, 2000). For example, in Liamputtong's book *Researching the Vulnerable* (2007), vulnerable people are defined as *"individuals who are marginalised and discriminated (sic) in society due to their social positions based on class, ethnicity, gender, age, illness, disability and sexual preferences"*. However, the categorisation of vulnerable groups does not substitute a definition of vulnerability (Carlier, 2017). For example, little to no scientific literature, nor human rights courts, such as the ECtHR or the Inter-American

Court of Human Rights, define what 'vulnerability' entails but make extensive use of the term in their jurisprudence (Rota, 2020).

Limiting the understanding of vulnerability to an enumeration of characteristics and subsequent needs is lacking in various aspects. Defining 'vulnerable groups' solely based on them sharing a characteristic leads to essentialism; it reduces said persons' complex identity to that one specific characteristic which is deemed 'vulnerable' (Fineman, 2013; Phillips, 2010). Furthermore, by solely focusing on individual characteristics, this understanding of vulnerability only highlights intrinsic factors (such as age, disability, physical and mental health) (Zimmermann, 2022). Consequently, an exclusive characteristic-based approach often fails to acknowledge structural factors which cause this vulnerability.

1.2 Context-based Understanding of Vulnerability

In order to move towards a more holistic understanding of vulnerability, it is crucial to take contextual factors into account. A context-based understanding of vulnerability rejects essentialist perspectives that simplify individuals or groups into predefined categories of vulnerability. Instead, it acknowledges that vulnerability is fluid and relational, arising from complex interactions between personal characteristics, situational, and systemic or structural factors (Blondel, 2015; Carlier, 2017; Soulet, 2014b, 2014c). Situational factors refer to a specific setting, such as prisons, whereas structural or systemic factors refer to broader societal dynamics (such as racism, sexism, ableism, xenophobia, homophobia, biphobia, transphobia and queerphobia…) (Blondel, 2015). A context-based approach towards vulnerability also recognises that these various factors are not isolated and can intersect with each other, resulting in unique forms of layered and compounded vulnerabilities (Crenshaw, 1991).

The context-based approach emphasises that vulnerability is not an inherent trait of certain individuals, but rather a result of unequal power dynamics and structural disadvantages present within a specific setting or society at large. As Blanc (2015: 154) states: *"Vulnerability is not fundamentally inherent to individuals but manifests itself in relation to their environment"*. In other words, incarcerated persons with specific characteristics are not vulnerable because of them having that characteristic; it is the lack of acceptance and adaptation of the context where they are put in which lies at the root of their increased likelihood to negative experiences and victimisation. According to Soulet (2014b, 2014c), it is therefore essential to understand vulnerability as originating from and interacting with the characteristics of the system (*in casu* prison with its own norms and ways of functioning) and the people who are part of said system (*in casu* other incarcerated people, prison staff and actors within the broader criminal justice system).

Because of its strong association with the notion of protection, focusing on vulnerability often results in identifying specific needs attributed to the categories of people considered as vulnerable (Soulet, 2014c). Prisoner victimisation research is no different; categories of incarcerated individuals who are more likely to report victimisation are often considered to have specific safety needs to mitigate this increased risk of victimisation. A context-based approach underscores the need for tailored interventions that account for the unique challenges faced by different categories of people in a well-defined context (Blondel, 2015; Le Blanc, 2019). As an example, this rationale lies at the basis of the United Nations Office on Drugs and Crime (UNODC, 2009) handbook on 'Prisoners with Special Needs' which discusses different categories of incarcerated persons considered as vulnerable (e.g. people with disabilities) and proposes specific interventions to mitigate this vulnerability (e.g. accessible infrastructure and accommodations to ensure their basic rights, such as having access to a common shower, work and activities). Because vulnerability and its resulting needs are a consequence of a complex interplay of distinct individual factors with contextual characteristics, context-based vulnerability extends the circle of people and authorities who are responsible for the protection of vulnerable persons (Zimmermann, 2022).

In this context-based approach towards vulnerability, the locus of responsibility for meeting these specific needs shifts from the individual to the state (Holder, 2018, 2022). When considering the state's responsibility towards vulnerable groups, a context-based perspective underscores the importance of meeting specific needs and challenges faced by these groups. By recognising and addressing specific needs, the state can work to alleviate the systemic factors contributing to vulnerability (Goodin, 1985a, 1985b). The state's positive obligation in recognising vulnerability and meeting specific needs is closely related to the concept of the welfare state, although it can be found in other state models (Goodin, 1985a, 1985b; Le Blanc, 2019). Just as a caregiver's duty involves tending to the unique needs of their recipients, the state's responsibility extends to addressing the diverse challenges faced by vulnerable people. The ECtHR has stated and reiterated the duty of the state to protect persons in custody because of their inherent vulnerability, and explicitly mentions the state's obligation to account for people part of 'particularly vulnerable groups' in prison because of their heightened risk of abuse (such as homosexual men, sexual offenders, police collaborators and former police officers).[1]

The context-based approach and its focus on state responsibility is also closely related to the ethics of care (as formulated by Gilligan (1982) and Tronto, (1993, 2009)), a moral framework that prioritises empathy, responsibility and interdependence. This ethical approach emphasises relationships and the moral obligation to provide care and support to those who are vulnerable. Very much like the ethics of care, a context-based understanding of vulnerability recognises the complexities of individuals' experiences and needs, as opposed to a limited characteristic-based understanding of vulnerability (Soulet, 2014d).

This specific attention to the complex interplay of individual characteristics while taking contextual factors into account will serve as a framework to discuss the vulnerability of incarcerated persons and the implications for prisoner victimisation research in the sections below.

---

[1] *Keenan v. The United Kingdom*, App. no. 27229/95, 3 April 2001, § 91; *Younger v. The United Kingdom*, decision as to the admissibility of App. no. 57420/00, 7 January 2003; *Trubnikov v. Russia*, App. No. 49790/99, 5 July 2005, § 68; *Renolde v. France*, App. no. 5608/05, 16 October 2008, § 83; *Jasińska v. Poland*, App. No. 28326/05, 1 June 2010, § 60; *De Donder and De Clippel v. Belgium*, App. no. 8595/06, 6 December 2011, § 70; *D. v. Latvia*, App. no. 76680/17, 11 January 2024, § 39; *Stasi v. France*, App. no. 25001/07, 20 October 2011, § 91; *J. L. v. Latvia*, App. no. 23893/06, 17 April 2012, § 68; *D. F. v. Latvia*, App. no. 11160/07, 29 October 2013, §§ 81–84; *M. C. v. Poland*, App. no. 23692/09, 3 March 2015, § 90; *Sizarev v. Ukraine*, App. no. 17116/04, 17 January 2013, §§ 114-115; *Totolici v. Romania*, App. no. 26576/10, 14 January 2014, §§ 48-49.

2 Vulnerable and Incarcerated, a Double Vulnerability?

The vulnerability of (certain categories of) incarcerated persons has been recognised on multiple occasions. Two layers of vulnerability can be distinguished: the institutional vulnerability of all incarcerated persons because of their status as prisoners, and the vulnerability of specific categories of incarcerated individuals linked to some of their identity characteristics. This section examines the use of the concept of 'vulnerability' when referring to incarcerated persons in general, and to well-defined categories. This ambiguity in the use of the term may lead to a different representation of vulnerable categories of incarcerated persons, as compared to other persons who are incarcerated.

2.1 All Incarcerated Persons Are Vulnerable, but Some Are More Than Others

The vulnerability of incarcerated persons because of their specific status has been generally recognised and accepted. The European Union explicitly mentions the vulnerability of incarcerated individuals in their EU 2020–2025 Strategy on victims' rights, based on the reported victimisation rates occurring in detention.[2] In ECtHR jurisprudence, the status of being detained is recognised as a source of vulnerability in and of itself[3] (Besson, 2014; Zimmermann, 2022). As a result of this acknowledged vulnerability, the ECtHR has stated multiple times that state authorities

---

[2] Communication from the Commission to the European Parliament, the Council, the European Economic and Social Committee and the Committee of the Regions. EU Strategy on Victim's Rights (2020–2025), COM(2020).
258, p. 14.
[3] Originally mentioned in *Aydin v. Turkey*, App. no. 23178/94, 25 September 1997, § 83. Recurring for example in *Slimani v. France*, App. no. 57671/00, 27 July 2004, § 27.

have the duty to protect incarcerated persons.[4] The contextual vulnerability considered as inherent to incarcerated persons can be defined as institutional vulnerability (Gordon, 2020). It stems from the fact that incarcerated individuals are under the formal authority of the prison administration and immediate prison staff for almost every aspect of their lives. This dependency results in a power imbalance and contributes to a specific kind of vulnerability because of the status of incarcerated persons within the penal institution. This dependency has also been recognised by the ECtHR (Zimmermann, 2015).[5]

Apart from institutional vulnerability, which is inherent to all incarcerated individuals, there is a lot of attention in human rights (soft) law and policy on specific categories of incarcerated persons who are distinctively labelled as 'vulnerable prisoners'. For example, the UNODC's (2009) handbook on 'Prisoners with Special Needs' enumerates the following categories of incarcerated people who are deemed as 'particularly vulnerable': people with mental healthcare needs, people with disabilities, ethnic and racial minorities and indigenous peoples, foreign national incarcerated persons, LGBTQ+ (lesbian, gay, bisexual, transgender and queer) people, older persons, people with terminal illness and people under sentence of death. The ECtHR also considers certain categories of incarcerated persons to be 'more vulnerable than the average detainee'.[6] This includes individuals in custody, incarcerated persons with a mental disability or suffering from mental illness, incarcerated persons with a physical disability, foreign detainees, incarcerated individuals who speak a different language than the authorities, incarcerated persons who committed sexual offences, ex-policemen, torture victims, minors, elderly incarcerated persons and pregnant women (Besson, 2014; Dehaghani, et al., 2023; Maillard, 2011; Zimmermann, 2022). The vulnerability of incarcerated women has also explicitly been recognised

---

[4] *Keenan v. The United Kingdom*, App. no. 27229/95, 3 April 2001, § 91; *Younger v. The United Kingdom*, decision as to the admissibility of App. no. 57420/00, 7 January 2003; *Trubnikov v. Russia*, App. No. 49790/99,5 July 2005, § 68; *Renolde v. France*, App. no. 5608/05, 16 October 2008, § 83; *Jasińska v. Poland*, App. No. 28326/05, 1 June 2010, § 60; *De Donder and De Clippel v. Belgium*, App. no. 8595/06, 6 December 2011, § 70.

[5] *De Donder and De Clippel v. Belgium*, op. cit.

[6] Formulation used in *Kudła v. Poland*, App. no. 30210/96, 26 October 2000, § 99.

by the United Nations, most visibly in their elaboration of the United Nations Rules for the Treatment of Women Prisoners and Non-custodial Measures for Women Offenders (the Bangkok Rules).[7]

The idea of identifying specific categories of incarcerated persons as being particularly vulnerable, has led several authors to speak of 'double vulnerability' (see for example Leghtas, 2016; Nuytiens & Christiaens, 2012; Turner et al., 2018; Van Hout & Crowley, 2021; Schlanger, 2017). The concept of double vulnerability sheds light on the compounded disadvantages experienced by specific categories of incarcerated persons within the criminal legal system by looking at the interaction between different identity characteristics and the contextual factor of being incarcerated. It thus combines institutional vulnerability with factors of social vulnerability. Social vulnerability is rooted in the systemic devaluation of the experiences and needs of specific categories of people (Gordon, 2020). By doing so, looking at 'double vulnerability' allows for an intersectional understanding of vulnerability in specific groups of incarcerated persons. When applied to the prison context, the concept of intersectionality (Crenshaw, 1991) contributes to understanding how particular categories of incarcerated individuals experience compounded vulnerabilities due to their overlapping marginalised identities and their status as a prisoner. For instance, foreign incarcerated persons in custody, incarcerated women of low socio-economic status, incarcerated LGBTQ+ individuals or persons with disabilities may face unique challenges.

2.2 Making Institutional Victimisation Visible

If all incarcerated persons are considered as vulnerable, what then is the relevancy of defining certain categories of incarcerated individuals as being more vulnerable? The recognition of the institutional vulnerability of incarcerated persons allows to broaden the scope of what is traditionally understood as victimisation to all kinds of harm experienced by incarcerated persons caused by the penal institution itself (Asquith et al.,

---

[7] Res 65/229 on the United Nations Rules for the Treatment of Women Prisoners and Non-custodial Measures for Women Offenders, adopted by the UN General Assembly on 21 December 2010.

2016). While prisoner victimisation studies often focus on victimisation experiences at the hands of other incarcerated persons or prison staff, the iatrogenic harm caused by institutional measures (such as differences in regime, isolation, inability to meet specific needs) is often less explicitly discussed (Asquith et al., 2016). Looking at institutional vulnerability in combination with the attention to specific categories of incarcerated persons, shifts the attention from interpersonal forms of victimisation to situational (prison-specific) and structural (systemic) factors which contribute to harmful experiences.

For example, incarcerated women may face increased risks of sexual abuse on an interpersonal level, but also experience inadequate access to reproductive healthcare and limited opportunities for rehabilitation tailored to their needs (Carlen & Worrall, 2004; CPT, 2018; Nuytiens & Christiaens, 2012). Incarcerated LGBTQ+ persons face an increased risk of harassment, abuse and discrimination from both fellow incarcerated people and prison staff due to structural dynamics (such as homophobia, biphobia, transphobia and queerphobia) (Beck et al., 2013; Blanc, 2015; Jenness et al., 2019; NCTE, 2018). At an institutional level, they might also be victimised by inappropriate staff behaviour during body searches, being put in long isolation as a protective measure and/or the lack of access to specific (psychological or gender-affirming) care (Donohue et al., 2021; Van Hout & Crowley, 2021; Vanliefde, 2023). Incarcerated persons with disabilities and elderly people might especially be affected by accessibility barriers, inadequate medical care or the lack thereof, and find themselves in a cycle of neglect and isolation (Humblet, 2021; Leghtas, 2016; Schlanger, 2017; Turner et al., 2018).

Within the field of prisoner victimisation research, it is important to acknowledge the growing body of literature where victimisation experiences are embedded within a broader assessment of the prison climate and context. Several studies researching the quality of life in prison include experiences of aggression and violence with a multitude of other factors related to the prison environment (architecture, regime, contacts between incarcerated persons and staff, physical well-being, feelings of safety…) and the prison climate (see Liebling et al., 2011, 2019; Skar et al., 2019; van Ginneken et al., 2018). Furthermore, prisoner victimisation has also been studied from a social control-opportunity framework

(Goossens & Daems, this volume; Steiner & Wooldredge, 2020). This approach to researching prisoner victimisation allows for a more nuanced and multifactorial understanding of dynamics leading to victimisation experiences, beyond focusing on single individual characteristics (see also Wilkinson, and van Ginneken, this volume).

3 Limitations of and Concerns Related to the Concept of Vulnerability

The concept of vulnerability allows to focus on certain groups of incarcerated persons who are more likely to experience victimisation, all the while broadening the scope of victimisation to iatrogenic harm caused by the prison as an institution, and structural harm by societal norms which marginalise certain groups. However, the use of the concept vulnerability has several limitations and generates concerns. Apart from the undefined and vague nature of the concept (see *supra*), three main risks related to the use of the term 'vulnerability' can be identified: the risk of essentialisation and oversimplification, the risk of further stigmatisation and the risk of paternalism and disempowerment (Peroni & Timmer, 2013; Zimmermann, 2022).

This reflection is important for the field of (prison) victimology, as (prisoner) victimisation studies can shape interventions in practice. By qualifying people as 'vulnerable' because they share a characteristic which is related to a higher likelihood of victimisation, victimisation studies form a theoretical basis for interventions and policy. In prison settings, interventions aimed at protecting 'vulnerable prisoners' merely by focusing on specific characteristics might be harmful, depending on how they are implemented. They run the risk of stigmatising and disempowering certain people, viewing them as a homogeneous group without recognising their differences, individual experiences of fear or harm and resilience (Heaslip et al., 2023; Spiers, 2000). By doing so, they fail to target situational factors within the prison which may cause or re-enforce the vulnerability of these persons. The limitations to and concerns regarding the use of the concept of vulnerability are discussed below.

3.1 Essentialism and Oversimplifying

One of the primary risks associated with using the concept of vulnerability is essentialism, whereby complex individuals or groups are reduced to a single defining characteristic and considered as a homogeneous group (Fineman, 2013; Phillips, 2010). Essentialism can lead to a reductionist perspective, obscuring the multifaceted nature of vulnerability and the intersectionality of numerous factors contributing to it. This is especially so in a characteristic-limited understanding of vulnerability. Focusing on one single characteristic erases individual differences within said category of people, often belonging to minorities, all the while exaggerating their difference with others (Fineman, 2013; Phillips, 2010; Zimmermann, 2022). The latter dynamic, the process of magnifying differences between people who do and don't belong to a minority group, is also called 'othering'.

By solely focusing on one aspect of vulnerability, such as age, gender or physical health, an essentialist understanding of vulnerability overlooks the intricate interplay of situational and structural factors that shape an individual's or group's susceptibility to victimisation or harm. This critique on essentialism was one of the foundations of the development of intersectional theory (Crenshaw, 1991). Peroni and Timmer's (2013) analysis of the ECtHR's case law also inspires caution to avoid actively creating vulnerable 'groups' of people, by defining them solely based on certain characteristics while neglecting individual differences. In practice, oversimplification hinders the development of effective strategies to mitigate vulnerability, as it fails to capture the complexity of individual situations. Regardless of them belonging to a category of incarcerated persons which is seen as vulnerable, individual needs might differ which makes an individual assessment necessary (Gatherer et al., 2014).

3.2 Stigmatisation

Secondly, the use of the concept of vulnerability can inadvertently perpetuate stigmatisation and marginalisation, processes which these categories of people already might have to endure. When vulnerability is framed as an inherent characteristic of a specific group of people, it risks reinforcing negative stereotypes and biases. In that sense, 'vulnerability' can act as a stigmatising label (Flohimont, 2020; Herring, 2016; Peroni & Timmer, 2013; Zimmermann, 2022). In terms of Goffman (1963), stigmatisation occurs when a certain identity characteristic is viewed as deviating from the societal norm and thus 'spoils' one's identity.

The process of stigmatisation is a relational one (Goffman, 1963): it occurs because of unconscious expectations and internalised norms, which in turn will shape behaviour and social interaction towards people labelled as 'vulnerable'. In a characteristic-based approach to vulnerability, the one targeted identity characteristic of a person might lead to a paradox of well-intentioned (legislative of policy) initiatives striving towards equity which ultimately stigmatise as a consequence (Flohimont, 2020; Herring, 2016). Applied to prison settings, this might lead to an increased visibility of vulnerable categories of prisoners due to targeted interventions, but also to segregation and isolation, albeit as a 'protective measure'. For example, McNaughton, Nicholls and Webster (2018) have found England and Wales's separate prison wings for incarcerated persons who committed sexual offences (Vulnerable Prisoner Units, VPU) to increase levels of stigmatisation and negative labelling as they 'mark' prisoners out as sexual offenders.

3.3 Paternalism and Disempowerment

The third significant concern related to the use of the concept of vulnerability, is the risk of paternalistic intervention and disempowerment. Imposing the label of 'vulnerability' on categories of people may lead those in position of authority to assume a paternalistic role in managing the vulnerability of others (Butler, 2014, 2016; Fineman, 2008, 2013; Herring, 2016; Timmer & Peroni, 2013). Paternalistic approaches can perpetuate a cycle of dependency, where marginalised individuals or groups are prevented from developing the skills and capacities necessary to address their own vulnerabilities (Blanc, 2015; Zimmermann, 2022). Such approaches do not take into account the self-perception of one's own vulnerability, the agency and the resilience of vulnerable individuals (Heaslip et al., 2023; Spiers, 2000). Instead, these top-down approaches fail to address the root causes of vulnerability (Butler, 2014, 2016; Herring, 2016; Peroni & Timmer, 2013; Zimmermann, 2022).

Butler (2019) also highlights the discursive power underlying the use of the term 'vulnerability' as the authorities or the ones in power ultimately decide who is considered vulnerable and who is not. Indeed, defining which categories of people are deemed vulnerable is predominantly dictated by experts (s.a. academics, practitioners and policymakers), sometimes silencing the individual experiences of vulnerability of the concerned persons (Heaslip et al., 2023; Parker et al., 2020). The label of 'vulnerability' might thus be imposed on or denied to specific categories of people. Within this paternalistic approach, 'vulnerability' is imposed on the targeted populations as a label, which is a display of discursive power in and of itself.

This can lead to disempowerment of the targeted populations deemed as 'vulnerable', as individuals or groups may be denied agency and the opportunity to participate in decision-making processes that affect their lives (Blanc, 2015; Butler, 2014, 2016, 2019; Zimmermann, 2022). Indeed, the consistent labelling of some categories of people as 'vulnerable' is closely related to the perception that they are incapable of self-determination or agency, contributing to a self-fulfilling prophecy where individuals or groups internalise this perception and fail to pursue opportunities for growth and empowerment (Bernardini, 2016, 2018; Butler, 2019).

This representation of vulnerability is inherently linked to a perception of fragility, weakness and lack of resilience (Bernardini, 2016, 2018). These representations are reminiscent of Christie's (1986) conceptualisation of 'the ideal victim', based on characteristics such as weakness, (young or older) age, respectability and blamelessness. Incarcerated persons generally are not regarded as victims, because they don't fit the imaginary concept of the 'ideal victim' (see Daems & Goossens in the introduction of this book). However, categories of incarcerated people labelled as vulnerable ones might be more likely to be recognised as victims than others, specifically because of the underlying assumption of lack of resilience and weakness which is inherent to both concepts of 'vulnerability' and the stereotypical representation of 'the ideal victim'.

3.4 A Binary Understanding of Vulnerability: Does Invulnerability Exist?

As discussed earlier in this chapter, specific categories of people can be labelled as 'vulnerable' because of their higher likelihood to experience harm. However, if some categories of people are considered vulnerable, does that mean that others are not? There is an inherent problem to a binary understanding of vulnerability, which is that invulnerability does not exist. Vulnerability functions differently from other combinations of terms which are each other's opposite (e.g. strong vs. weak; normal vs. deviant); it is impossible to oppose 'vulnerability' to 'invulnerability' applied to real-life situations (Soulet, 2014c).

Furthermore, a binary understanding of vulnerability presents a risk of a hierarchisation of victims and their needs (Jankovitz, 2018; Zimmermann, 2022). This hierarchisation occurs when the needs of people recognised as being (particularly) vulnerable, which often belong to minorities, seemingly become more important than others who are not recognised as vulnerable. The same happens with ranking certain categories of people into a 'victim hierarchy', based on how deserving they are of the victim status based on (1) the perception of guilt or innocence and the use of violence; (2) political and media representations and attention to specific groups of people; (3) pragmatic rankings based on an assessment of the amount of harm done and/or (4) a group's self-perception of the status as a victim within the 'victim-offender' dichotomy as opposed to their perception of another group of people (Jankovitz, 2018). While incarcerated people do not conform to the stereotype of 'the ideal victim', as conceptualised by Nils Christie (1986), certain characteristics associated with vulnerability (e.g. being young or old age, gender, people with disabilities) can play into the recognition of these groups as 'more deserving' victims. While this can be the result of a rebalancing exercise in the attention given to specific groups which were previously neglected, the intent of focusing on this group cannot be to retrograde the needs of other groups. Creating a hierarchy in victim status and their needs is also inherent to the power dynamics in defining who is vulnerable and who is not (Butler, 2019). This discursive power also entails a sense of merit, as defining who is vulnerable and who is not implies a differentiation in practice of who is more deserving of protection and having their needs met.

This finding led certain philosophers, such as Fineman (2008, 2013) and Nussbaum (2001, 2006), to consider that vulnerability, to some extent, is universal and inherent to human beings. When looking at incarcerated persons, the fact that some specific categories of them are deemed 'particularly vulnerable' does not do away with the recognition that all incarcerated persons are vulnerable to some extent because of their dependency on prison authorities. As Zimmermann (2022) argues, vulnerability must be understood as a continuum, rather than a characteristic which is present or absent or a fixed label put on an individual. Vulnerability depends on specific personal and contextual conditions, some of which are likely to change over the lifetime of a person.

3.5 When Theory Informs Practice: More Harm Than Good?

The concept of vulnerability serves as an important lens through which to understand and address personal, situational and structural characteristics which can lead to prisoner victimisation. However, risks of essentialism, stigmatisation and paternalism emerge with the use of the term 'vulnerability', as discussed earlier in this section. Prisoner victimisation studies can inform penal policy by identifying vulnerable categories of incarcerated individuals, which is why a careful consideration of these concerns is necessary. Indeed, policies inspired by results from prisoner victimisation studies can lead to categorising entire groups of incarcerated persons as being (particularly) vulnerable because of certain identity characteristics. However, targeted interventions merely based on one single personal identity characteristic (such as age or disability) fail to recognise and tackle situational and structural factors contributing to their vulnerability (Holder, 2018, 2022). By focusing on a single characteristic, such interventions are fundamentally lacking to act upon the multitude of intersecting identity characteristics of an individual which contribute to that person's vulnerability (Markarian, 2023). Going further, characteristic-specific interventions might even be instrumentalised within a strategy to mask iatrogenic characteristics of the prison as an institution which contributes to victimisation. For example, support groups or separate wings for specific categories of vulnerable incarcerated individuals may be promoted as a legitimate effort to tackle vulnerabilities of this specific category of incarcerated persons but does not address the lack of tolerance from other incarcerated individuals and prison staff which lies at the root of their victimisation experiences. Furthermore, advocating for the creation of separate units for 'vulnerable' incarcerated individuals can be an argument to promote building new facilities. In that sense, researchers, policymakers and practitioners must be aware that highlighting the vulnerability of certain groups of incarcerated persons can be utilised an argument to segregate these persons in separate units within a broader movement of carceral expansion (Markarian, 2023).

While penal policies and practices targeted at specific categories of incarcerated persons might be useful to meet specific needs which are otherwise overlooked, they run an important risk of further stigmatising and disempowering these people by imposing the label 'vulnerable'. This is where prison authorities might find themselves facing a dilemma. Developing specific policies on vulnerable categories of incarcerated persons might contribute to meeting certain specific needs but might also make them even more visible. For example, consider a counselling group for incarcerated individuals who are victims of sexual abuse, or a support group for LGBTQ+ people, where they must disclose this personal information in order to participate. This forced outing of personal information can lead to an increased visibility and ultimately more victimisation experiences for the very people the intervention was supposed to protect. This paradox is why, in some cases, prison authorities might choose not to put specific measures in place considering vulnerable groups to limit this visibility and risk of victimisation cycle. Indeed, penal policies meant to reduce the vulnerability of certain categories of incarcerated individuals, might not actually provide the intended pathways to safety and inclusion (see Maycock, 2022 for an example of issues with the Scottish policy on incarcerated transgender persons). This is especially so when prison authorities fail to recognise and/or tackle the structural factors (such as racism, sexism, ableism, queerphobia) which underlie these victimisation experiences. As a last resort, prison authorities might have to resort to isolation as a protective measure for vulnerable incarcerated individuals. While this recognises the higher risk of victimisation of some incarcerated persons and is meant to provide protection, it is a form of institutional violence in and of itself. Segregating entire groups of incarcerated persons from the general population (as incarcerated women are separated from men, or categories of incarcerated individuals reside in so-called 'protected sections' or Vulnerable Prison Units) may ultimately be one of the only interventions with immediate result in trying to reduce risks of victimisation. However, segregating entire groups of people deemed as 'vulnerable' and limiting contact with other incarcerated persons enhance the risk of them having less access to parts of the prison infrastructure, work and activities, which negatively impacts them.

While the attention to the vulnerability of certain categories of incarcerated persons, often belonging to minorities, may be viewed by prison staff as disproportionate, interventions designed to limit harm and victimisation may in fact benefit the entire prison population. For example, measures aimed at reducing risks of victimisation during body searches can be beneficial to respect the dignity of all incarcerated individuals, even if these measures were initially taken to meet the specific safety needs of vulnerable incarcerated persons (Vanliefde, 2023). This might include having multiple members of staff present to monitor each other's behaviour, having a register of searches, allowing the person undergoing the search to remain partly clothed during the search or putting a functional complaint mechanism in place for incarcerated persons. This illustration shows that it remains important to report on vulnerability in prisoner victimisation research in a nuanced and context-based manner which allows to recognise the complex interplay of factors leading up to vulnerability and mitigate the risks of hierarchisation of needs, essentialisation, stigmatisation, paternalism and disempowerment discussed in this chapter.

4   Conclusion

The concept of 'vulnerability' has extensively been used in different fields over the last decades, from legal studies and philosophy to social sciences. In prisoner victimisation research, vulnerability is often used to refer to identity characteristics of incarcerated persons who experience higher rates of victimisation. The term allows to broaden the scope of what is traditionally understood as victimisation by uncovering situational (specific to the prison context) and structural (discrimination present at societal level) factors which contribute to victimisation. By looking at situational and structural factors interacting with personal characteristics, a context-based understanding of vulnerability may contribute to identifying and acting upon specific needs of categories of incarcerated persons who are more likely to suffer harm. A significant amount of recent studies (namely on prison climate) include prisoner victimisation within an integrated framework of contextual factors, offering a more nuanced and multifaceted understanding of the vulnerability and victimisation experiences of incarcerated persons (see also the respective chapters of Goossens and Daems, Wilkinson, and van Ginneken in this book).

The vulnerability of all incarcerated persons has been recognised in literature, policy documents and in jurisprudence. This institutional vulnerability stems from their dependency of prison authorities and staff for almost every aspect of their lives. The recognition of institutional vulnerability renders the state responsible for protecting incarcerated persons, and especially categories of them who are more likely to be harmed in prison. Converging with institutional vulnerability, some incarcerated individuals are deemed to be 'particularly vulnerable' because of personal characteristics such as age, ethnicity, gender identity, sexual orientation, illness or disability, which increase the likelihood of victimisation.

Too narrow of an understanding of vulnerability, which only focuses on one or more personal characteristics, entails several risks. First, there is a risk of essentialisation, where the complex identity of incarcerated individuals is reduced to that one characteristic which is deemed vulnerable. Second, labelling incarcerated persons as vulnerable can be experienced as stigmatising. Making minority characteristics visible by disproportionately focusing on them can lead to negative and harmful behaviour from other incarcerated individuals and prison staff, or to interventions with negative or harmful outcomes (such as isolation as a means of protection, or segregation). Finally, imposing the label of 'vulnerability' on entire categories of people, without any regards to individual differences, dispossess them of their agency and misrecognises their own perception of their vulnerability and their resilience. This may contribute to a paternalistic attitude towards vulnerable categories of incarcerated persons, where prison authorities are the ones managing their vulnerability without necessarily considering the preferences, individual differences and toughness of these individuals. Indeed, there is a (discursive) power dynamic inherent to the labelling of categories of people as vulnerable, a power which researchers, policymakers and practitioners should particularly be aware of. This chapter is not intended to dissuade researchers, practitioners and policymakers from using the concept of vulnerability. Instead, it aims to highlight the nuances and implications of the concept and invite to reflect on the use of the term 'vulnerability' in prisoner victimisation studies. In this power also lies the potential for research on prisoner victimisation to shed the light on structural deficiencies and for practitioners to tackle them, all the while recognising the differences and resilience of categories of incarcerated persons considered as vulnerable.

References

Asquith, N. L., Bartkowiak-Theron, I., & Roberts, K. (2016). Vulnerability and the criminal justice system. *Journal of Criminological Research, Policy and Practice, 2*(3), 161–163. https://doi.org/10.1108/JCRPP-06-2016-0009

Beck, A.J., Berzofsky, M, Caspar, R., & Krebs, C. (2013). *Sexual victimization in prisons and jails reported by inmates, 2011–12*. Bureau of Justice Statistics. https://bjs.ojp.gov/content/pub/pdf/svpjri1112.pdf

Bernardini, M. G. (2018). « Dangerous liaisons ». Critical reflections on vulnerability, disability and law. *Sociologia Del Diritto, 1*, 101–123. https://doi.org/10.3280/SD2018-001005

Bernardini M.G. (2016). Vulnerability and the (disability) law: Status, challenges and promises of a controversial category. *Gênero & Direito, 5*(3), 132–151. https://doi.org/10.18351/2179-7137/ged.v5n3p132-151

Besson, S. (2014). La vulnérabilité et la structure des droits de l'homme: l'exemple de la jurisprudence de la Cour européenne des droits de l'homme. In L. Burgorgue-Larsen (Ed.), *La vulnérabilité saisie par les juges en Europe* (pp. 59–85). Pedone.

Blanc, J.-S. (2021). *La prise en charge des personnes LGBTIQ+ en détention*. Centre Suisse de Compétences en matière d'exécution des Sanctions Pénales CSCSP. https://www.unige.ch/cmcss/application/files/3316/2558/3714/Document_cadre_La_prise_en_charge_des_personnes_LGBTIQ_en_detention.pdf

Blanc, J.-S. (2015). Minorités sexuelles en détention: De l'invisibilité à la stigmatisation. In N. Queloz, T. Noll, L. von Mandach, & N. Delgrande (Eds.), *Vulnérabilité et risques dans l'exécution des sanctions pénales* (pp. 149–171). Stämpfli Verlag.

Blondel, M. (2015). *La personne vulnérable en droit international* (PhD thesis). Université de Bordeaux.

Boone, M., Althoff, M., Koenraadt, F., & Timp, I. (2016). *Het leefklimaat in justitiële inrichtingen*. WODC.

Brodiez-Dolino, A. (2014). La vulnérabilité, une notion opératoire pour penser l'enfance en danger? In L. Lardeux (Ed.), *Vulnérabilité, identification des risques et protection de l'enfance. Nouveaux éclairages croisés* (pp. 11–21). La Documentation Française.

Burgorgue-Larsen L. (2014). La vulnérabilité saisie par la philosophie, la sociologie et le droit. De la nécessité d'un dialogue interdisciplinaire. In L. Burgorgue-Larsen (Ed.), *La vulnérabilité saisie par les juges en Europe* (pp. 237–239). Pedone.

Butler, J. (2019). Bodies that still matter. *Raisons Politiques, 76*(4), 15–26. https://doi.org/10.3917/rai.076.0015

Butler, J. (2016). Rethinking vulnerability and resistance. In J. Butler, Z. Gambetti, & L. Sabsav (Eds.), *Vulnerability in resistance* (pp. 9–19). Duke University Press.

Butler, J. (2014). Bodily vulnerability, coalitions, and street politics. *Critical Studies, 37*, 97–119. https://doi.org/10.1163/9789401210805_007

Carlen, P., & Worrall, A. (2004). *Analysing Women's Imprisonment* (1st ed.). Willan. https://doi.org/10.4324/9781843924210

Carlier, J.-Y. (2017). Des droits de l'homme vulnérable à la vulnérabilité des droits de l'homme, la fragilité des équilibres. *Revue Interdisciplinaire d'Études Juridiques, 79*(2), 175–204. https://doi.org/10.3917/riej.079.0175

Chamberland, L., & Saewyc, E. (2011). Stigma, vulnerability, and resilience: The psychosocial health of sexual minority and gender diverse people in Canada. *Canadian Journal of Community Mental Health/revue Canadienne De Santé Mentale Communautaire, 30*(2), 1–5. https://doi.org/10.7870/cjcmh-2011-0012

Christie, N. (1986). The ideal victim. In E. A. Fattah (Ed.), *From Crime Policy to Victim Policy* (pp. 17–30). Palgrave Macmillan.

Clément, M., & Bolduc, N. (2004). Regards croisés sur la vulnérabilité: Le politique, le scientifique et l'identitaire. In M. Clément, F. Saillant, & C. Gaucher (Eds.), *Identités, vulnérabilités, communautés* (pp. 61–82). Nota Bene.

Cohen, S. (1989). The critical discourse on "social control": Notes on the concept as a hammer. *International Journal for the Sociology of Law, 17*(3), 347–357.

Crenshaw, K. (1991). Mapping the margins: Intersectionality, identity politics, and violence against women of color. *Stanford Law Review, 43*(6), 1241–1299. https://doi.org/10.2307/1229039

Dehaghani, R., Fairclough, S., & Mergaerts, L. (2023). *Vulnerability, the accused, and the criminal justice system*. Routledge.

Donohue, G., McCann, E., & Brown, M. (2021). Views and experiences of LGBTQ+ people in prison regarding their psychosocial needs: A systematic review of the qualitative research evidence. *International Journal of Environmental Research and Public Health, 18*(17), 1–17. https://doi.org/10.3390/ijerph18179335

Committee for the Prevention of Torture and Inhuman or Degrading Treatment or Punishment (CPT). (2018). Factsheet on women in prison. *Cpt/inf, 2018*, 5.

Faberon, F. (2014). Vulnérabilité et besoin dans le droit de l'aide et de l'action sociales. In E. Paillet & P. Richard (Eds.), *Effectivité des droits et vulnérabilité de la personne* (pp. 49–60). Bruylant.

Fineman, M. A. (2013). Equality, autonomy and the vulnerable subject in law and politics. In M. A. Fineman & A. Grear (Eds.), *Vulnerability: Reflections on a new ethical foundation for law and politics* (pp. 13–28). Ashgate Publishing Limited.

Fineman, M. A. (2008). The vulnerable subject: Anchoring equality in the human condition. *Yale Journal of Law and Feminism, 20*(1), 1–23.

Flohimont, V. (2020). Le droit ne stigmatise-t-il pas les individus en voulant accueillir la vulnérabilité à tout prix? In D. Doat, & L. Rizzerio (Eds.), *Accueillir la vulnérabilité. Approches pratiques et questions philosophiques* (pp. 151–186). Érès.

Gatherer, A., Atabay, T., & Hariga, F. (2014). Prisoners with special needs. In S. Enggist, L. Møller, G. Galea, & C. Udesen (Eds.), *Prisons and health* (pp. 151–158). World Health Organization.

Gilligan, C. (1982). *In a different voice: Psychological theory and women's development*. Harvard University Press.

Goffmann, E. (1963). *Stigma: Notes on the management of spoiled identity*. Prentice-Hall Inc.

Goodin, R. E. (1985a). *Protecting the vulnerable*. The University of Chicago Press.

Goodin, R. E. (1985b). Vulnerabilities and Responsibilities: An ethical defense of the welfare state. *The American Political Science Review, 79*(3), 775–787. https://doi.org/10.2307/1956843

Gordon, B. G. (2020). Vulnerability in research: Basic ethical concepts and general approach to review. *The Ochsner Journal, 20*(1), 34–38. https://doi.org/10.31486/toj.19.0079

Heaslip, V., Dugdale, C., Parker, J., Johnsen, B., & Hean, S. (2023). Experiences of vulnerability in adult male prisoners: An integrative review. *The Prison Journal, 103*(1), 122–153.

Herring, J. (2016). *Vulnerable adults and the law*. Oxford University Publishers.

Holder, R. (2022, June 6). *Beyond vulnerability: re-conceiving victims as citizens*. [Keynote presentation]. 17th International Symposium of the World Society of Victimology, San Sebastian.

Holder, R. (2018). *Just interests: Victims, citizens and the potential for justice*. Edward Elgar Publishing.

Humblet, D. (2021). *The older prisoner*. Palgrave Macmillan.

Jankowitz, S. E. (2018). *The order of victimhood: Violence, hierarchy and building peace in Northern Ireland*. Palgrave Macmillan.

Jenness, V., Sexton, L., & Sumner, J. (2019). Sexual victimization against transgender women in prison: Consent and coercion in context. *Criminology, 57*(4), 603–631. https://doi.org/10.1111/1745-9125.12221

Johnsen, B., Rokkan, T., Liebling, A., Beyens, K., Boone, M., Kox, M., Schmidt, B., & Vanhouche, A-S. (2017). *Measuring the Quality of Life* at Norgerhaven prison. KRUS. https://brage.bibsys.no/xmlui/handle/11250/2497200

Le Blanc, G. (2019). Qu'est-ce que s'orienter dans la vulnérabilité? *Raisons Politiques, 76*(4), 27–42.

Leghtas, I. (2016). *Double punishment. Inadequate conditions for prisoners with psychosocial disabilities in France.* Human Rights Watch. https://www.hrw.org/report/2016/04/05/double-punishment/inadequate-conditions-prisoners-psychosocial-disabilities.

Levinas, E. (1998). *Otherwise than being or beyond essence (translated by Alphonso Lingis).* Kluwer Academic Publishers.

Liamputtong, P. (2007). *Researching the vulnerable: A guide to sensitive research methods.* Sage.

Liebling, A., Hulley, S., & Crewe, B. (2011). Conceptualising and Measuring the Quality of Prison Life. In D. Gadd, S. Karstedt, & S. Messner (Eds.). *The SAGE Handbook of Criminological Research Methods* (pp. 358–372). Sage. https://doi.org/10.4135/9781446268285

McNaughton Nicholls, C., & Webster, S. (2018). *The separated location of prisoners with sexual convictions: Research on the benefits and risks.* HM Prison & Probation Service.

Mackenzie, C., Rogers, W., & Dodds, S. (2014). *Vulnerability: New essays in ethics and feminist philosophy.* Oxford University Press.

Maillard, N. (2011). *La vulnérabilité. Une nouvelle catégorie morale?* Éditions Labor et Fides.

Markarian, Q. (2023, September 20). *L'impossible « prison inclusive ». Regard queer abolitionniste sur la catégorisation carcérale des personnes trans.* [Paper presentation]. Seminar "Penser les catégories pénales à l'aune des sciences sociales".

Maycock, M. (2022). The transgender pains of imprisonment. *European Journal of Criminology, 19*(6), 1521–1541. https://doi.org/10.1177/1477370820984488

National Center for Transgender Equality. (2018). *LGBTQ people behind bars: A guide to understanding the issues facing transgender prisoners and their legal rights.* NCTE. https://transequality.org/sites/default/files/docs/resources/TransgenderPeopleBehindBars.pdf

Nussbaum, M. C. (2001). *The Fragility of Goodness: Luck and Ethics in Greek Tragedy and Philosophy* (2nd ed.). Cambridge University Press.

Nussbaum, M. C. (2006). *Frontiers of Justice. Disability, Nationality, Species Membership.* Harvard University Press.

Nuytiens, A., & Christiaens, J. (2012). Female offenders' pathways to prison in Belgium. *Temida, 15*(4), 7–22. https://doi.org/10.2298/TEM1204007N

Parker, J., Heaslip, V., Ashencaen Crabtree, S., Johnsen, B., Hean, S., Hean, S., Johnsen, B., Kajamaa, A., & Kloetzer, L. (2020). People in contact with criminal justice systems participating in service redesign: vulnerable citizens or democratic partners. In *Improving collaboration, innovation and organisational learning in penal systems* (pp. 297–322). Palgrave Macmillan

Phillips, A. (2010). What's wrong with essentialism? *Distinktion: Scandinavian journal of social theory, 11*(1), 47–60. https://doi.org/10.1080/1600910X.2010.9672755

Peroni Manzoni, M. L., & Timmer, A. (2013). Vulnerable groups: The promise of an emerging concept in European Human Rights Convention law. *International Journal of Constitutional Law, 11*(4), 1056–1085. https://doi.org/10.1093/icon/mot042

Rota, M. (2020). La vulnérabilité dans la jurisprudence de la Cour européenne et de la Cour interaméricaine des droits de l'homme. *Cahiers De La Recherche Sur Les Droits Fondamentaux, 18*, 39–46. https://doi.org/10.4000/crdf.6422

Ruet, C. (2015). La vulnérabilité dans la jurisprudence de la Cour européenne des droits de l'homme. *Revue Trimestrielle Des Droits De L'homme, 102*, 317–340.

Schlanger, M. (2017). Prisoners with disabilities. In E. Luna (Ed.), *Reforming criminal justice: Punishment, incarceration, and release* (pp. 295–323). Academy for Justice.

Skar, M., Lokdam, N., Liebling, A., Muriqi, A., Haliti, D., Rushiti, F., & Modvig, J. (2019). Quality of prison life, violence and mental health in Dubrava prison. *International Journal of Prisoner Health, 15*(3), 262–272. https://doi.org/10.1108/IJPH-10-2017-0047

Soulet M.-H. (2014a). La vulnérabilité, une ressource à manier avec prudence. In L. Burgorgue-Larsen (Ed.), *La vulnérabilité saisie par les juges en Europe* (pp. 7–29). Pedone.

Soulet, M.-H. (2014b). Les raisons d'un succès. La vulnérabilité comme analyseur des problèmes sociaux contemporains. In I. Brodiez-Dolino, B. Von Bueltzingsloewen, B. Eyraud, B. Ravon, & C. Laval (Eds.), *Vulnérabilités sanitaires et sociales, de l'histoire à la sociologie* (pp. 59–64). Presses universitaires de Rennes

Soulet M.-H. (2014c). Vulnérabilité et enfance en danger. Quel rapport? Quels apports? In L. Lardeux (Ed.), *Vulnérabilité, identification des risques et protection de l'enfance. Nouveaux éclairages croisés* (pp. 128–139). La Documentation Française.

Soulet, M.-H. (2014d). *Vulnérabilité: de la fragilité sociale à l'éthique de la sollicitude*. Academic Press Fribourg.

Spiers, J. (2000). New perspectives on vulnerability using emic and etic approaches. *Journal of Advanced Nursing, 31*(3), 715–721. https://doi.org/10.1046/j.1365-2648.2000.01328.x

Steiner, B., & Wooldredge, J. (2020). *Understanding and reducing prison violence*. Routledge.

Timmer, A. (2013). A quiet revolution: Vulnerability in the European Court of Human Rights. In M. A. Fineman & A. Grear (Eds.), *Vulnerability: Reflections on a new ethical foundation for law and politics* (pp. 147–170). Ashgate Publishing Limited.

Turner, M., Peacock, M., Payne, S., Fletcher, A., & Froggatt, K. (2018). Ageing and dying in the contemporary neoliberal prison system: Exploring the 'double burden' for older prisoners. *Social Science & Medicine, 212*, 161–167. https://doi.org/10.1016/j.socscimed.2018.07.009

Turner, B. S. (2006). *Vulnerability and human rights*. Penn State University Press.

Tronto, J. (2009). *Un monde vulnérable. Pour une politique du care*. Éditions La Découverte.

Tronto, J. C. (1993). *Moral boundaries: A political argument for an ethic of care*. Routledge.

United Nations Office for Drugs and Crime. (2009). *Handbook on prisoners with special needs*. UNODC.

van Ginneken, E. F. J. C., Palmen, H., Bosma, A. Q., Nieuwbeerta, P., & Berghuis, M. L. (2018). The Life in Custody study: The quality of prison life in Dutch prison regimes. *Journal of Criminological Research, Policy and Practice, 4*(4), 253–268. https://doi.org/10.1108/JCRPP-07-2018-0020

Van Hout, M. C., & Crowley, D. (2021). The 'double punishment' of transgender prisoners: A human rights-based commentary on placement and conditions of detention. *International Journal of Prisoner Health, 17*(4), 439–451. https://doi.org/10.1108/IJPH-10-2020-0083

Vanliefde, A. (2023). Body searches and vulnerable groups: Women and LGBTQI+ people in prison. In T. Daems (Ed.), *Body searches and imprisonment* (pp. 101–129). Palgrave Macmillan.

Zimmermann, N. (2022). *La notion de vulnérabilité dans la jurisprudence de la Cour européenne des droits de l'homme. Contours et utilité d'un concept en vogue* (PhD thesis). Schulthess Verlag.

Zimmermann, N. (2015). Legislating for the vulnerable? Special duties under the European Convention on Human Rights. *Swiss Review of International and European Law, 23*(2), 539–562.

Methodological Challenges in Victimisation Studies

Elien Goossens

In recent years, the victimisation of prisoners has come to be studied more widely, including in research using quantitative methodology. However, much of this research suffers from a lack of standardisation of measurement methods and methodological intransparency, making national and cross-country comparisons virtually impossible. Yet we know from research on psychological and cognitive processes that certain methods in questionnaire design are better than others. Studies on victimisation are also susceptible to additional risks and pitfalls, such as nonresponse, which may be amplified in a prison context. This chapter reviews the problems in prior research and the unique challenges in designing a victimisation study for prisoners. It draws on a review of the methodological literature and our practical experiences with conducting a study on prisoners' victimisation in Flanders (for a discussion of this study, see elsewhere in this volume: Goossens & Daems) to formulate

E. Goossens (✉)
Leuven Institute of Criminology (LINC), KU Leuven, Leuven, Belgium
e-mail: elien.goossens@kuleuven.be

recommendations for a better standardisation of questionnaire design and data collection in prison victimisation studies.

In the first section, we explore subject and operationalisation challenges, specifically focusing on the formulation of victimisation questions and how respondents can be involved in questionnaire design to achieve culturally relevant measurements. Following, we address various technical measurement challenges: the use of reference periods, answer options and the ordering of topics and questions. The chapter concludes with a discussion of (non)response challenges and strategies for researchers to deal with them. Several of the recommendations discussed in this chapter are based on the findings from the Flemish study (Goossens & Daems, this volume). Drawing from the topics covered, a questionnaire was developed to assess self-reported incidents of prisoner-on-prisoner victimisation. Referred to as '*The Detention Monitor*', this questionnaire is available open access for reference (see Goossens & Daems, 2023).

1   Subject and Operationalisation Challenges

Researchers often face critical questions when it comes to measuring prisoners' victimisation. For example, they need to decide whether to ask questions about specific incidents or to use general, open question formats. Another choice is whether to use a combined construct scale or not. Recognising the interplay between victimisation and the specific country or institutional context, it is also essential to tailor measurements accordingly. A further challenge lies in the absence of clear definitions and frameworks. How to proceed in the absence of such guidance becomes an important consideration. Therefore, this section tries to address these questions and offers some recommendations.

1.1 Behavioural Versus General Questioning

In previous studies, researchers have applied varying definitions to measure prisoners' victimisation. Some researchers have approached this by employing a general question, asking whether the individual has experienced an assault or has been victimised (e.g. Caravaca-Sánchez et al., 2019; Hensley et al., 2005; Listwan et al., 2014). This strategy often requires asking one question, such as: '*Since you have been incarcerated, has another inmate sexually assaulted you?*' (Hensley et al., 2005) or '*Have you been physically assaulted by [inmate or staff] in the previous 6 months?*' to assess physical victimisation (Caravaca-Sánchez et al., 2019). Although using general questions in victimisation surveys offers the advantage of a shorter questionnaire, allowing for the inclusion of additional questions on the situational context of the victimisation or perpetrators, it is important to acknowledge three significant drawbacks associated with this approach (*cf.* Table 1).

First, the use of general terms such as 'victimisation' or 'assault' in questionnaires can lead to varying interpretations among respondents. As noted by Wolff et al. (2007), not all individuals in prison immediately identify incidents like beatings as falling under the definition of victimisation. In a study on the effect of (harsh) parenting on misbehaviour in detention, Klatt and Kliem (2021) observed that respondents' self-assignment of their victimisation status might have influenced survey results. This issue was also reported in the research conducted by Rufino et al. (2013) on gang members, where the researchers formulated a hypothesis that certain violent incidents tended to be normalised among gang members, leading to underreporting in their study. It is essential to recognise that the **subjective experience of victimhood** varies among individuals and some may not perceive themselves as victims, even after experiencing a criminal incident.

An illustration of the impact of questioning format on victimisation measurement can be found in Wolff et al.'s (2006) study. The researchers found that using behavioural items in questionnaires yielded higher prevalence rates compared to general questioning. More specifically, prevalence rates for sexual victimisation were lower when using a general question ('*Have you been sexually assaulted by an inmate or staff*

Table 1 Overview of advantages and disadvantages of using behavioural and general questions

Behavioural questioning		General questioning	
Advantages	*Disadvantages*	*Advantages*	*Disadvantages*
Reduced subjective interpretation	Longer questionnaire: More emotional and cognitive burden for respondents less space for additional background questions	Shorter questionnaire: Reduced emotional and cognitive burden for respondents, more space for background questions	Open to subjective interpretation
Results in detailed information on specific incidents, allows the measurement of various incidents within one victimisation type	Risk of measuring 'trivial' or 'normalised' incidents in some respondents' views (e.g. insults) and therefore respondent drop-out		Provides less information on specific incidents
Allows researchers to differentiate between victimisation types	Requires a pre-test and respondent interviews to identify relevant behavioural items		Risk of measuring victimisation types as one concept (e.g. physical and sexual violence, verbal threats and physical incidents)

member within the past 6 months?') compared to ten behavioural questions (e.g. unwanted touching, forced sex, etc.), with only 23 per 1000 female prisoners reporting sexual victimisation. When behavioural questions were used, the number of reported sexual cases increased to 210 per 1000 female prisoners. Among male prisoners, the prevalence of sexual victimisation was 16 per 1000 prisoners with the general question and rose to 38 per 1000 prisoners when using behavioural questions. These findings were consistent with other research on physical victimisation (Wolff et al., 2007').

Second, adopting general questions and terminology in surveys poses the risk of **combining victimisation types**. For example, when a questionnaire includes the term 'assaults' respondents are left to determine whether this encompasses both physical, non-sexual assaults and sexual assaults, or if it only refers to physical incidents. A lack of differentiation between victimisation types is problematic, as researchers have identified varying risk factors depending on different types of violence (e.g. Wooldredge & Steiner, 2014). In addition, studies found different prevalence rates of victimisation depending on whether the perpetrator is a fellow inmate or a staff member (Caravaca-Sánchez & Wolff, 2016; Wolff et al., 2006). For this reason, it is not only recommended to distinguish between various forms of victimisation but also to specify the perpetrator in the questioning, depending on the research focus (*'another inmate'* or *'staff member'*, as opposed to *'anyone'*, *'someone'* or no specification at all).

Last, general questions offer **little or no information** about the specific incidents of victimisation that occur in prison. When prevalence rates are measured, the researcher gains no insight into the nature or form of the reported circumstances. It is therefore recommended to measure victimisation through specified behavioural items. However, quite a few researchers have recognised the importance of behavioural items and still arrived at various measurements. Wolff and colleagues, for example, examined physical victimisation by questioning if prisoners had experienced one or more of the following incidents that related to inmate-on-inmate fights: being (1) slapped, hit, kicked or bitten, (2) choked or attempted to drown, (3) hit with some object, (4) beaten up and (5) threatened or harmed with a knife or shank (e.g. Blitz et al., 2008; Caravaca-Sánchez & Wolff, 2016; Wolff & Shi, 2009a; Wolff et al., 2022). Other researchers who have adopted behavioural items added injuries or physical harm to the definition (e.g. *'Since your admission, have you been injured in a fight, assault, or incident in which someone tried to harm you?'*) (e.g. Daquin & Daigle, 2021; Howard et al., 2020; Meade et al., 2021; Toman, 2019; Wood & Buttaro, 2013). Moreover, different behavioural items are being applied across studies. Measuring victimisation solely as physical harm is problematic because not every incident necessarily results in physical harm. There is a risk here of 'non-inclusiveness': not all potential behavioural items that fall under physical victimisation are surveyed. The same applies to studies of sexual victimisation where the focus is sometimes solely on rape and touching, overlooking other forms of hands-off sexual victimisation, such as harassment and verbal sexual violence (e.g. Vertommen et al., 2016 for an overview of behavioural items on sexual victimisation and other violence types). However, there is also the risk of adopting items that are only relevant within specific regions and cultures. For example, studies conducted in countries like Taiwan and South Korea included behavioural items such as not being allowed to sleep, forced to get tattoos and being immersed in water (Kuo et al., 2014; Reyns et al., 2018). While these items may be culturally relevant in those countries, they could be of lesser relevance in other countries. Moreover, behavioural items may not only be irrelevant to the context but can also include incidents that respondents perceive as trivial, for example, when swear words or threats are strongly normalised in the prison culture (Ireland & Qualter, 2008; Muehlenhard et al., 2017). Both irrelevant and trivial items can lead to respondent dissatisfaction and drop-out. Here, researchers should consider the trade-off between gathering as much relevant information as possible and the potential of respondent drop-out. This consideration may depend on whether the objective is to measure objective numerical figures of incidents, which may sometimes seem banal to respondents, or to measure subjective perceptions of victimisation. In the light of these considerations, there is also a growing demand for a framework or inclusive behavioural definition of victimisation.

1.2 The Problem of Region and Culture

Although much research on victimisation in prisons has traditionally been conducted in the US, we can observe that more recently studies have been undertaken in many other countries, including Spain, Germany, Belgium, UK, Taiwan and South Korea (e.g. Caravaca-Sánchez & Wolff, 2017; Choi, 2019; Goossens & Daems, this volume; Neubacher, 2020; Kuo et al., 2021; Warren & Jackson, 2012; Wilkinson & Fleming, 2021). It should not come as a surprise that prison systems and cultures differ from country to country, or even within countries (see, e.g., Coyle, 2021). Prisons are microsocieties with specific sets of values and social structures (Sykes, 1958). Against this background victimisation incidents, as documented in research, may also take different shapes, depending on the context of the study.

This does not only apply to the measurement of prisoners' victimisation but also the decision on what background questions to ask for risk factor analyses. For example, concepts related to gang affiliation and ethnicity may have different interpretations and relevance depending on the region. In the US, it seems reasonable to differentiate between Hispanics, Latinos, blacks and whites but in other countries, other ethnicities will be more relevant. Factors such as the size of the prison population, the type of activities for prisoners, prison officer culture and staffing levels, human rights and complaint procedures may all vary and thus affect victimisation differently.

1.3 Framework and Definitions of Prisoners' Victimisation

Defining prisoners' victimisation can be very challenging. The first step is to acknowledge the **distinction between victimisation types**. In an American ethnographic study, Bowker (1980) identified four forms of prisoners' victimisation: physical, sexual, psychological and economic victimisation.[1] Previous research has highlighted that non-physical victimisation incidents are reported more frequently than physical incidents (e.g. Caravaca-Sánchez & Wolff, 2018; Edgar et al., 2003) and yet there is still a predominant focus on sexual and physical victimisation. In addition to measuring multiple victimisation types, it is also essential to analyse each victimisation type separately. For instance, in

---

[1] Additionally, Bowker referred to social victimisation when victims are targeted because of a certain group membership. Social victimisation, however, can encompass physical, sexual, psychological and economic forms.

some studies threats are included under the definition of physical victimisation (e.g. Hensley et al., 2005; McGrath et al., 2012; Wolff & Shi, 2009b), whereas it could be argued that a threat without any physical attack should be considered a form of psychological victimisation.

Second, the use of behavioural items within questionnaires raises the question if a **latent construct scale** should be designed based on these items. While this approach is employed in some studies (e.g. Kuo, 2019), where reasonable factor loadings and internal reliability are reported, working with a construct scale seems less favourable. For example, in a recent study Kuo (2019) transformed a scale of physical victimisation into a binary 'yes/no' variable to conduct logistic regression analyses in determining risk factors, meaning that prisoners who had experienced at least one of the incidents were categorised as victims. This approach was also logical, because when utilising a latent construct scale to assess victimisation, it is assumed that victimisation is a theoretical construct comprised of various items that together reflect the otherwise unobservable nature of victimisation (DeVellis, 2017). However, if the research objective is to measure factual incidents rather than the subjective identification of prisoners who have been victimised, combining individual items into a construct scale becomes unnecessary. In principle, incidents can be directly observed. While correlations might exist between items (for instance, someone experiencing insults may also face threats), it is plausible that separate incidents could happen and a person could be considered a victim (of one incident). In this context, adopting the binary 'yes/no' approach is appropriate when the aim is to measure the prevalence rates of factual incidents, instead of understanding if prisoners personally perceive themselves as victims.

Our discussion so far has demonstrated that it is a challenge to arrive at an inclusive operationalisation which allows for differentiation and is at the same time not overly specific. Overall, the choice of behavioural items will depend on the national, local and cultural background, which implies that variations in the measurement across national boundaries and time will always be present. Nevertheless, information can be gathered and lessons can be learnt from previous studies to make international comparative research possible.

1.4 Think Aloud

Questionnaire design should be partially **participant-driven** (Charters, 2003; Trenor et al., 2011). In this regard, the think-aloud methodology by Ericsson and Simon (1980) can be helpful. Think aloud is a qualitative research methodology in which respondents are asked to verbalise their thoughts while completing a questionnaire. The goal is to discover potential issues in understanding, memory retrieval, decision making and answering questions (Collins, 2003; Dietrich & Ehrlenspiel, 2010). More precisely, the verbalisation of thoughts during questionnaire completion helps researchers to determine whether respondents interpret and answer survey items as intended. Additionally, it can help with the identification of survey items which may be perceived as irrelevant or missing by respondents within their specific (prison) context. Overall, researchers have two options in conducting think-aloud interviews: they can either refrain from any interventions and only observe, or take a more interactive approach by using probes and interventions (Ji & Rau, 2019). Although some researchers recognise that the interactive approach to think aloud may cause distraction and can be cognitively demanding for respondents (Hertzzum, 2009), the approach has the advantage of allowing the researcher to seek clarification from participants. Moreover, asking questions might feel more natural for respondents (Zhao & McDonald, 2010). Examples of think-aloud probes and interventions can be found in several studies (e.g. Collins, 2003; Olmsted-Hawala et al., 2010; Trenor et al., 2011; Zhao & McDonald, 2010). Table 2 gives a selective overview of probes and interventions during thinking aloud.

However, the think-aloud method can be quite demanding: the participant does most of the talking, shifting the burden from the researcher to the respondent (Collins, 2003). Additionally, think aloud can be an uncomfortable or unnatural experience, as people typically do not verbalise their thoughts aloud (Alhadreti & Mayhew, 2018). Furthermore, the method relies on verbal reporting while not all cognitive processes can be verbalised. Some processes occur so rapidly that they leave no trace in working memory. This method can also be more challenging for individuals who are less articulate (Collins, 2003). Therefore,

Table 2 Examples of probes and interventions during think aloud

General probes	Specific interventions
Keep talking Continue thinking aloud What are you thinking about?	What do you think this question is asking? What does this word mean to you? What is your opinion of the items being asked under this topic? What do you think of the language here? How did you arrive at this answer? How did you remember that?
Observational interventions	*Retrospective interventions*
I noticed you hesitated before you answered. What were you thinking about? You changed your answer. What made you change it?	What is your general opinion of the questionnaire? What do you think of the subject/content of the topics? What suggestions do you have for improvement?

observing non-verbal signals can contribute to the method (Charters, 2003). Examples of non-verbal signals include moments of silence, body movements, variations in vocal tone, changing answers and taking time to read questions. Additionally, the researcher can conduct a retrospective interview on the evaluation of the questionnaire after the think-aloud process.

2 Technical Measurement Challenges

Technical considerations in questionnaire design involve the length of the reference period to be used, response options, and the order of items in questions.

2.1 Reference Period

The timeframe within which respondents are required to recall events for reporting is referred to as the reference period (Lynch & Addington, 2010). Using reference periods helps to reduce ambiguity in questioning and simplifies the task for respondents (Lavrakas, 2008), as the question provides more context for the recall task. On the one hand, Wolff et al. (2008) propose shorter reference periods for prison studies, as prisoners frequently transfer between facilities. On the other hand, Wolff et al. (2008) suggest that longer reference periods would be more suitable for capturing infrequent occurrences like sexual victimisation. This is due to the increased likelihood of these events being remembered more effectively, as well as the difficulty of measuring these rarer occurrences within research that utilises shorter reference periods (Clarke et al., 2008; Kjellsson et al., 2014).

Incidents of physical violence are usually easier remembered over longer time periods of time because of the **saliency** or seriousness of such incidents (Lynch & Addington, 2010). Saliency refers to the resonance or 'impact' of an event on a person, indicating its significance in their life. Such incidents are therefore notable, evoke stronger emotions and are more exceptional, resulting in a more accurate recall. In contrast, non-exceptional incidents and/or incidents with presumably lower saliency, such as emotional violence (insults, threats, etc.) in prison, are less easily remembered over a longer reference period (Lavrakas, 2008; Lynch & Addington, 2010). Due to temporal memory effects and memory decay, prisoners often do not accurately recall the timing and consequently the frequency of these 'ordinary' events (Lavrakas, 2008; Wooldredge & Steiner, 2013). Likewise, it is more challenging to recall how many times one went to the supermarket in the past 6 months compared to how many times one ended up in the emergency room of a hospital in the same period. As a result, respondents may unintentionally report victimisation incidents that fall outside the reference period (overreporting) or conversely, they may fail to report incidents that do fall within the reference period (underreporting), a phenomenon known as telescoping (Clarke et al., 2008). In short, the advice is to use a shorter reference period for incidents with presumably lower saliency and to employ a longer reference period for incidents with presumably higher saliency (Lavrakas, 2008). Nonetheless, when the study focuses on various types of victimisation with varying degrees of saliency, it is necessary to select a single reference period in order to facilitate meaningful comparisons among the different victimisation types.

Many studies seem to adopt a reference period of 6 months. However, one might ask whether a reference period of 6 months is still too long when it comes to recalling the frequency of emotional and economic victimisation. Moreover, if physical victimisation is quite common within the prison subculture, as has been documented in previous studies (e.g. Caravaca-Sánchez & Wolff, 2016; Wolff et al., 2007), there are good reasons to consider using shorter reference periods (e.g. 2 months, see Martens et al., 2021, Goossens & Daems, this volume). This would also offer advantages for questioning pre-trial detainees and prisoners with short sentences who often spend less than 6 months in their current prison. Conversely, if researchers are studying hands-on sexual violence, a longer reference period might be recommended. In such cases, however, the study would need to almost exclusively focus on hands-on offences. Hands-off sexual incidents, such as inappropriate sexual remarks and jokes, would be better studied using a shorter reference period, assuming that such incidents might occur more frequently. To conclude, it seems appropriate to opt for a reference period of 2 months when at least a significant portion of the studied victimisation types involves hands-off incidents (theft, vandalism, threats, insults, sexual remarks, exclusion, etc.). However, if the main focus of the study is on hands-on physical and sexual violence, then a 6-month interval seems to be the more appropriate.

2.2 Answer Options and Frequency Questions on Victimisation

In some victimisation studies, the frequency of victimisation is surveyed to obtain a measurement of repeated or multiple victimisation. Answer options to frequency questions can take on the format of either vague quantifiers or numeric quantifiers. **Vague quantifiers** involve respondents indicating the frequency of the event using concepts like 'rarely', 'sometimes' and 'often'. In contrast, **numeric quantifiers** refer to quantities, such as 'once', 'two to three times' and so forth (Gallhofer & Saris, 2007; Rocconi et al., 2020). Disadvantages of numeric quantifiers are related to memory effects, such as forgetting or telescoping (Tourangeau et al., 2000). Moreover, respondents might think that the researcher has chosen meaningful options and that the middle option reflects the population norm against which they can measure themselves (Krosnick, 2018; Schwarz, 1999).

However, with vague quantifiers, respondents need to interpret the concept behind the vague quantifier. For instance, one person might not assign the same numeric value to the word 'sometimes' compared to another person (Tourangeau et al., 2000; Wright et al., 2022). The reference group that respondents consider also influences answers when choosing vague quantifiers. In a study by Wänke (2002), students estimated higher cinema visit frequencies when comparing themselves to the whole population, unlike those comparing to fellow students. This implies that providing a comparison group might partly resolve ambiguity. However, this was contradicted by another study. Walentynowicz et al. (2022) tested vague and numeric quantifiers, varying contextualisation by instructing respondents to a) compare with average adults or b) friends of their age or c) no comparison. This study found no association between the provided reference groups and the answers to vague and numeric quantifiers. It is possible that someone's perception of, for example, 'the average adult' or their friends is also subjectively biased by experiences. As Wright et al. (1994) observed, a person's perception of the frequency of TV consumption in an 'average person' positively correlates with their own TV behaviour.

It can be concluded that vague quantifiers lead to question ambiguity related to the meaning of concepts, which increase the risk of incorrect answers. Additionally, the discussed studies do not suggest that a reference group adequately reduces the ambiguity in vague quantifiers. Despite the known drawbacks of inaccurate memories, the frequency of victimisation should best be measured using numeric quantifiers in a closed response format. Nevertheless, researchers should weigh the value of measuring the frequency of victimisation against the cognitive burden it imposes on respondents. A substantial body of research exists that, despite offering frequency response categories, converts the victimisation outcome variable into a binary variable (either 'never experienced' or 'experienced at least once') due to low occurrences within categories indicating 'more than one time' (e.g. Goossens & Daems, this volume; Goossens et al., 2023; Martens et al., 2021; McNeeley, 2022). Therefore, if frequency holds less significance in relation to the broader research goal, it can be considered to omit frequency answer options and instead opt exclusively for yes/no answer options ('Yes, experienced at least once', 'No, never experienced').

2.3 Order of Topics and Questions

Regarding the sequence of topics and questions at least two key issues arise. The first is about the arrangement of demographic questions in the questionnaire. Generally, demographic questions are better suited for the start, allowing respondents to acclimatise and transition progressively to more complex topics (Babbie & Maxfield, 2015). Sensitive questions, such as questions on victimisation, are advised to be positioned towards the end (Dillman et al., 2014).

Two empirical studies in particular are relevant here. Drummond et al. (2008) explored two versions of a questionnaire on prostate cancer testing among 1458 healthcare workers: one with general demographic information followed by topic-specific questions (version 1) and the other with specific questions followed by demographic details (version 2). Results showed version 1 had a significantly higher response rate than version 2, possibly due to less (cognitively) demanding initial demographic questions facilitating a gradual shift towards more challenging topics (Drummond et al., 2008). Teclaw et al. (2012) examined overall response rates and the correlation between the placement of demographic questions on the one hand and item responses for demographic and non-demographic questions on the other hand. Placing demographic questions at the start of the survey led to a higher item response rate on those questions, possibly due to respondent fatigue towards the end. It might also reduce hesitance about providing demographic data as opposed to when more sensitive and personal questions (on opinions, experiences, etc.) are asked first. Moreover, placing demographic questions at the start or the end does not seem to significantly influence the item response rate on the non-demographic questions (Teclaw et al., 2012). Reflecting on the end of the questionnaire is equally important.

Several authors recommend inserting threatening topics, such as victimisation, between less intimidating ones to minimise perceived heaviness and underreporting (Bradburn et al., 2004; Dillman, 2007; Lee, 1999). Ethically, ending with a sensitive question on victimisation is unadvised. The recommendation is to adopt an 'easing out' strategy, gently concluding the survey, for example by including questions about prison and detention situation towards the end.

The second aspect is the sequence of chosen victimisation behavioural items. These items can be gradually ordered by their level of severity or mixed randomly. Randomising the order can counter consistency effects, for example when respondents tend to select 'never experienced' without reading the individual items. A gradual item sequence might also frustrate non-victimised participants, as they might view the progressively intensifying items as redundant (Straus et al., 1996). Ramirez and Straus (2006) studied the effect of item sequence on the reporting of partner violence using the Conflict Tactics Scales (CTS). The initial CTS assigned a 'culturally recognisable' sequence, moving from socially accepted behaviours (e.g. discussing the conflict with partner) to violence. Later, CTS2 randomised the order. Presenting both versions to 417 students, Ramirez and Straus (2006) observed higher violence and victimisation reporting with CTS2 (20% severe violence) than CTS1 (8%). Similar results appeared in prior research regarding the Beck Depression Inventory (BDI), where female students' responses to a randomly ordered BDI resulted in higher pathological scores than the standard, gradual order (Dahlstrom et al., 1990). Although these studies have small samples and focus on pathological symptoms and violent behaviour, they suggest random orders offer advantages over severity-based orders by reducing underreporting and potentially countering consistency effects (Chan et al., 2015).

3   Data Collection and Recruitment Challenges

In terms of data collection, researchers should keep in mind at least three elements. First, the cooperation of **prison officers** is imperative to facilitate physical access to the subjects under study. Efficient movement within the prison is significantly influenced by the quality of the relationship with prison staff. The role of prison officers extends beyond ensuring the safety of the researchers; they also need to feel motivated to efficiently guide the research team to various locations within the prison (Apa et al., 2012). Additionally, prison staff can impact response rates and the establishment of positive relationships with prisoners. For instance, officers might open cell doors more aggressively and impatiently under time pressure, as opposed to being friendly and respectful, leaving a different impression on the prisoners. Furthermore, discrepancies can arise between the time schedule for the data collection, as agreed upon by prison management, and the hours that prison officers in the wings are available. While obtaining permission from management and senior staff is important, it is prison staff in the wings, who have an understanding of the daily prison organisation, who will play a vital role in determining the researchers' work schedule for data collection. Therefore, maintaining open and fair communication about the study and the researcher's role are important.

Second, another group to consider is the **prisoners**. From the first day of data collection, the researcher's presence becomes known. Therefore, a good strategy is to positively engage prisoners. For example, in a recent Dutch prison study, researchers have discussed with representatives from prisoners' committees to disseminate information about the study's objectives (van Ginneken et al., 2018). In many facilities, there are a small number of prisoners who hold positions of responsibility and influence and these individuals can be approached to help spread the word about the study. They can further serve as prisoners' representatives to express concerns and share questions from fellow prisoners.

Third, each prison has its own **culture and regime**. The greatest challenge lies in comprehending the respective systems and finding adapted ways to operate within them (Byrne, 2005). For instance, in some prisons, researchers may have more freedom of movement across different sections, while this might not be permissible in other prisons. Researchers in closed institutions also rely on and need to adjust to daily routines within the organisation, such as scheduled walks, work and other programmes. To avoid disrupting daily operations, working on Sundays or evenings might be the most appropriate approach, both to not interfere with prison staff's duties and to have the opportunity to interact with the majority of prisoners.

Being aware of and addressing these three elements is part of an approach known as **ethnographic data collection**. Ethnographic data collection involves respectfully engaging with respondents, viewing them as study consultants and informants. They can offer feedback on research instruments and data collection strategies (e.g. think aloud), as well as provide valuable knowledge of the system they daily live in (Byrne, 2005). In a Dutch study, for example, researchers have personally recruited prisoners, for example at their prison cells (van Ginneken et al., 2018). This can be referred to as 'total population sample', where every member of the prison is personally invited to participate in the study by the research team. While this is a time-consuming and intensive approach, it allows for better response rates because prisoners know the faces of the research team, are usually better informed and have gained oral information on ethical procedures (e.g. response rates of 81% in the Dutch study on prison climate (van Ginneken et al., 2018)).

4 (Non)response Challenges

(Non)response and item nonresponse are common challenges when working with self-report surveys. However, in prison settings, such challenges can become even more difficult to deal with. Consider, for example, prisoners who move to another prison cell, get released or transferred to another prison, or pre-trial prisoners who change between and within facilities.

To address these challenges, the earlier mentioned approach to implement personal recruitment strategies may help, where researchers invite prisoners to participate in their study through face-to-face interactions and informed consent. In our study (Goossens & Daems, this volume), researchers visited prisons in person and distributed questionnaires at prison cell doors, with the goal of collecting them within a two-day timeframe. However, due to practical constraints within the prison system (partly due to COVID-19 restrictions), this personalised approach was not always feasible. In certain prisons, prison officers were tasked with distributing and collecting surveys. In other prisons, researchers were granted permission for one direct visit to the prison cells, but prisoners were required to return their completed questionnaires through the mail, for free. Response rates tended to be higher in prisons where the research team could carry out recruitment and personally collected the questionnaires at the cell doors. This was in contrast to the strategies where questionnaires had to be distributed by staff or collected through the mail. For example, compare the response rates of correctional prison 1 (25.81%) and mixed prison 6 (39.13%) with correctional prison 9 (6.17%) and mixed prison 13 (14.95%). Additionally, obtaining responses from pre-trial prisons was overall challenging (e.g. pre-trial prison 12; 10.30%) (see Table 3). The pre-trial prisoner population is more volatile and transient, resulting in questionnaire loss, or such prisoners might be less interested in participating due to personal concerns.

Based on these observations, it is recommended to adopt personal recruitment strategies and leave a maximum of two days between distribution and collection. When shorter time frames were adopted in a pilot study proceeding the abovementioned Flemish study (Goossens & Daems, this volume), working prisoners often complained that they did not have time to complete their questionnaire. In pre-trial prisons, however, recollection within a day or even on the same day of distribution is suitable due to less prison labour and activities in those facilities. In addition to personal recruitment, adherence to ethical procedures can contribute to an increase in the overall response rate. Engaging in personal, verbal recruitment enables researchers to explain the study's objectives but also to emphasise the costs and benefits of participation, helping prisoners in making informed decisions regarding their participation. Common disadvantages associated with participation in victimisation studies include the potential for respondents to feel uncomfortable or experience retraumatisation (e.g. Crowther & Lloyd-Williams, 2012; Israel, 2015; Lee, 1999). There is also the risk of retaliation from offenders (Jones & Pratt, 2008), the potential for stigmatisation of the population based on published research findings in the media (Roffee & Waling, 2017) and the possibility that prisoners participate due to perceived external pressures, such as the hope that participation will improve their image with prison staff or participation to reduce the feeling of social isolation (Dalen & Jones, 2010; Moser et al., 2004). Verbally explaining the measures taken to ensure confidentiality, repeating the voluntary character of the study, addressing the risks involved and demonstrating sensitivity as a researcher—such as providing contact information for counselling within the prison at the end of questionnaires—are essential elements of an ethics plan and can foster trust with respondents.

Item nonresponse occurs when respondents choose not to answer specific questions. Evidence from our study indicates that apart from sensitive questions (e.g. those related to drug use in prison), items that are more cognitively demanding also suffer from nonresponse. For example, the questionnaire incorporated two questions regarding the duration of time served. The first question asked, '*How long have you been in this prison without interruption?*', while the second asked, '*How long have you been in a prison without interruption?*'. The distinction between these two questions was that the first referred exclusively to the time spent in the current prison during the current detention, whereas the second aimed to capture the time spent in any prison during the current detention. However, the second question caused confusion (e.g. less served time in total compared to in the current prison) and therefore resulted in one of the highest percentages of missing data (8,7%) (*cf.* Fig. 1). Similarly, when prisoners were asked about the total number of detentions ('*How many times did you stay in prison as an adult (18 +), including the current detention?*'), this led to numerous unanswered questions (9,4%). In some cases, prisoners may also not know what their exact detention situation is, and are confused about the status of their

Table 3 Overview of retrieved questionnaires and response level in a Flemish study on prisoner-on-prisoner victimisation (Goossens & Daems, this volume)

Prison	Start DC	End DC	Prison population	Retrieved questionnaires	Response rate
Correctional prison(1)	11/11/2021	21/01/2022	403	104	25,81%
Pre-trial prison(2)	15/09/2022	30/09/2022	149	19	12,75%*
Correctional prison(3)	20/11/2021	22/11/2021	299	65	21,74%
Correctional prison(4)	07/01/2022	13/01/2022	288	39	13,54%**
Correctional prison(5)	27/11/2021	29/11/2021	183	64	34,97%
Mixed prison(6)	12/12/2021	13/12/2021	230	90	39,13%
Mixed prison(7)	22/05/2022	21/06/2022	595	168	28,24%
Correctional prison(8)	13/02/2022	13/02/2022	56	27	48,21%
Correctional prison(9)	23/02/2022	03/03/2022	227	14	6,17%**
Mixed prison(10)	06/03/2022	31/03/2022	717	202	28,17%
Pre-trial prison(11)	26/05/2022	28/05/2022	137	25	18,25%
Pre-trial prison(12)	01/08/2022	24/08/2022	660	68	10,30%
Mixed prison(13)	21/07/2022	04/08/2022	281	42	14,95%*
Total			4225	927	21,94%

* Partially personal recruitment: retrieval of questionnaire through mail
** No personal recruitment

case in court, or the offences they are accused or convicted of. Consequently, two recommendations are proposed to address the issue of item nonresponse. First, researchers can try to obtain prisoners' consent to access administrative data files. This was, for example, successfully done in a study in the Netherlands (e.g. Martens et al., 2021; van Ginneken et al., 2018). This approach allowed Dutch researchers to collect accurate background information while also reducing the length of the questionnaire. Moreover, this strategy may facilitate potential future longitudinal measurements that track a sample over time, surpassing the limitations of cross-sectional studies. However, implementing this approach requires approval from senior prison management, governments and ethical boards, has to be practically feasible and requires linking questionnaires to prisoners' personal files or identification numbers. In instances where these conditions cannot be met, a second recommendation involves confining background questions to only what is strictly necessary to the research objectives and excluding questions that are cognitively demanding.

5 Conclusion and Recommendations

This chapter addressed a range of challenges and pitfalls involved in conducting research on prisoner victimisation using quantitative questionnaires. A set of recommendations to questionnaire design and data collection approaches have been formulated, which can be summarised as follows:

Questionnaire Design:

- Conduct a literature review and examine existing instruments.
- Differentiate between various types of victimisation: physical, sexual, emotional and economic.
- Formulate items for behavioural incidents (e.g. have you been insulted?).
- Aim for inclusivity (e.g. measure hands-on and hands-off sexual victimisation, theft and vandalism).
- Choose a short reference period (e.g. 2 months) for studying all victimisation types; a longer reference period (e.g. 6 months) is suitable for only studying severe physical victimisation types.
- Avoid applying frequency answer options when they are less relevant to the research objective; yes/no answer options are less cognitively demanding.
- Avoid sensitive background questions; avoid cognitively demanding questions.

- Ease in and ease out: Begin with non-intrusive demographic background questions, then address victimisation topics and conclude with non-invasive questions about the detention situation.
- Pre-test the instrument to ensure alignment with the specific prison culture(s) under study, involving potential research participants (e.g. utilising think-aloud techniques).

Data Collection:

- Discuss with prison management, prison officers and influential prisoners to explain the study and determine the most feasible recruitment strategies.
- Schedule data collection during weekends and evenings to avoid prisoners being absent in their cells and to minimise extra workload for prison staff.
- Apply personnel recruitment strategies and survey recollection, and total population sampling whenever feasible. Retrieve surveys within a maximum of two days.
- Prioritise ethical considerations, including voluntary participation, informed consent, providing referrals for (psychological) support within the prison (particularly if the topic is sensitive) and think through a debriefing strategy for both prisoners and prison staff (Fig. 1).

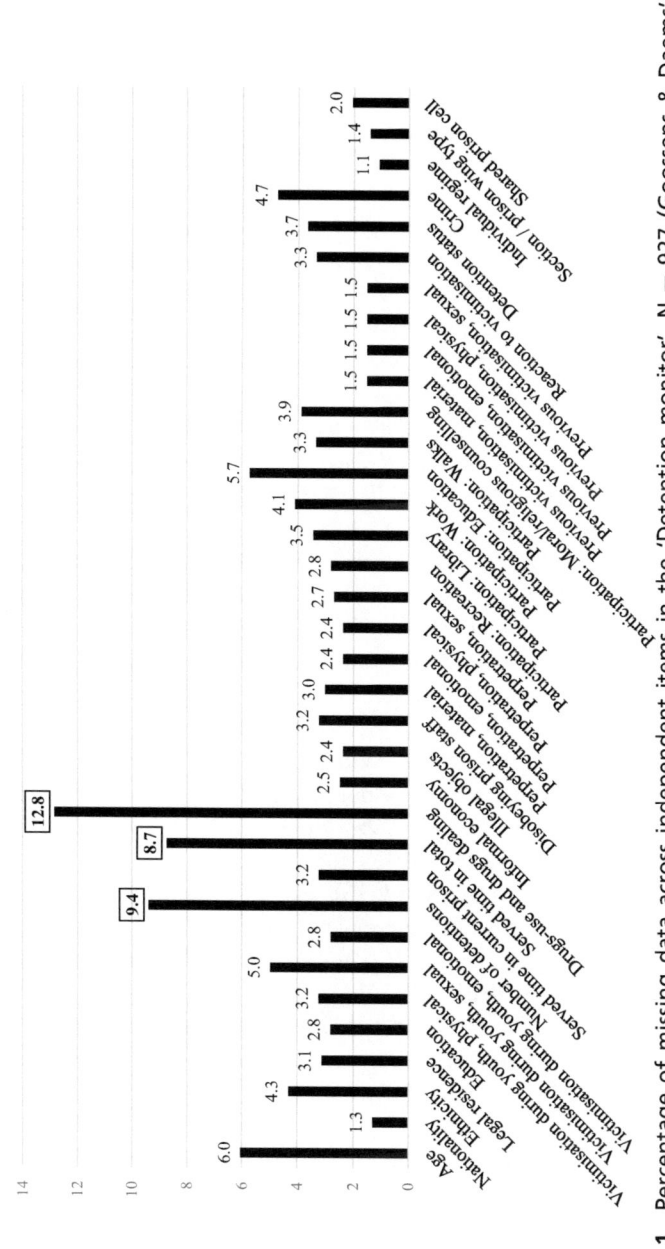

Fig. 1 Percentage of missing data across independent items in the 'Detention monitor', N = 927 (Goossens & Daems' study, this volume)

References

Alhadreti, O., & Mayhew, P. (2018). Rethinking thinking aloud: A comparison of three think-aloud protocols. CHI Conference on human factors in computing systems. https://dl.acm.org/doi/https://doi.org/10.1145/3173574.3173618

Apa, Z. L., Bai, R., Mukherejee, D. V., Herzig, C. T. A., Koenigsmann, C., Lowy, F. D., & Larson, E. L. (2012). Challenges and strategies for research in prisons. *Public Health Nursing, 29*(5), 467–472. https://doi.org/10.1111/j.1525-1446.2012.01027.x

Babbie, E. R., & Maxfield, M. G. (2015). *Research methods for criminal justice and criminology*. Cengage Learning.

Blitz, C. L., Wolff, N., & Shi, J. (2008). Physical victimization in prison: The role of mental illness. *International Journal of Law and Psychiatry, 31*(5), 385–393. https://doi.org/10.1016/j.ijlp.2008.08.005

Bowker, L. H. (1980). *Prison victimization*. Elsevier.

Bradburn, N. M., Sudman, S., & Wansink, B. (2004). *Asking questions: The definitive guide to questionnaire design for market research, political polls, and social and health questionnaires*. Jossey-Bass.

Byrne, M. W. (2005). Conducting research as a visiting scientist in a women's prison. *Journal of Professional Nursing, 21*(4), 223–230. https://doi.org/10.1016/j.profnurs.2005.05.001

Caravaca-Sánchez, F., Fearn, N. E., Vidovic, K. R., & Vaughn, M. G. (2019). Female prisoners in Spain: Adverse childhood experiences, negative emotional states, and social support. *Health & Social Work, 44*(3), 157–166. https://doi.org/10.1093/hsw/hlz013

Caravaca-Sánchez, F., & Wolff, N. (2016). Self-report rates of physical and sexual violence among Spanish inmates by mental illness and gender. The Journal of Forensic Psychiatry & Psychology, 27(3), 443–458. https://doi.org/10.1080/14789949.2016.1145721

Caravaca-Sánchez, F., & Wolff, N. (2017). The association between substance use and physical victimization among incarcerated men in Spanish prisons. *International Journal of Law and Psychiatry, 50*, 9–16. https://doi.org/10.1016/j.ijlp.2016.09.006

Caravaca-Sánchez, F., & Wolff, N. (2018). Understanding polyvictimization in prison: Prevalence and predictors among men inmates in Spain. *Journal of Interpersonal Violence, 1–27*,. https://doi.org/10.1177/0886260518775751

Chan, D. K., Ivarsson, A., Stenling, A., Yang, S. X., Chatzisarantis, N. L., & Hagger, M. S. (2015). Response-order effects in survey methods: A randomized controlled crossover study in the context of sport injury prevention. *Journal of Sport and Exercise Psychology, 37*(6), 666–673. https://doi.org/10.1123/jsep.2015-0045

Charters, E. (2003). The use of think-aloud methods in qualitative research an introduction to think-aloud methods. *Brock Education, 12*(2), 68–82. https://doi.org/10.26522/brocked.v12i2.38

Choi, J. (2019). Victimization, fear of crime, procedural injustice and inmate misconduct: An application of general strain theory in South Korea. *International Journal of Law, Crime and Justice, 59*, 1–12. https://doi.org/10.1016/j.ijlcj.2019.100346

Clarke, P. M., Fiebig, D. G., & Gerdtham, U.-G. (2008). Optimal recall length in survey design. *Journal of health economics, 27*(5), 1275–1284. https://doi.org/10.1016/j.jhealeco.2008.05.012

Collins, D. (2003). Pretesting survey instruments: An overview of cognitive methods. *Quality of Life Research, 12*(3), 229–238. https://doi.org/10.1023/A:1023254226592

Coyle, A. (2021). *Prisons of the world*. Bristol university press.

Crowther, J. L., & Lloyd-Williams, M. (2012). Researching sensitive and emotive topics: The participants' voice. *Research Ethics Review, 8*(4), 200–211. https://doi.org/10.1177/1747016112455887

Dahlstrom, W. G., Brooks, J. D., & Peterson, C. D. (1990). The Beck Depression Inventory: Item order and the impact of response sets. *Journal of Personality Assessment, 55*(1–2), 224–233. https://doi.org/10.1080/00223891.1990.9674062

Dalen, K., & Jones, L. Ø. (2010). Ethical Monitoring: Conducting research in a prison setting. *Research Ethics Review, 6*(1), 10–16. https://doi.org/10.1177/174701611000600103

Daquin, J. C., & Daigle, L. E. (2021). The victim–offender overlap in prison: Examining the factors associated with group membership. *Journal of Interpersonal Violence, 36*(23–24), NP13439–NP13462. https://doi.org/10.1177/0886260519898427

DeVellis, R. F. (2017). *Scale development: Theory and applications*. Sage.

Dietrich, H., & Ehrlenspiel, F. (2010). Cognitive interviewing: A qualitative tool for improving questionnaires in sport science. *Measurement in Physical Education and Exercise Science, 14*(1), 51–60. https://doi.org/10.1080/10913670903455025

Dillman, D. A. (2007). *Mail and internet surveys: The tailored design method.* Wiley.

Dillman, D. A., Smyth, J. D., & Christian, L. M. (2014). *Internet, phone, mail, and mixed-mode surveys: The tailored design method* (4th ed.). Wiley.

Drummond, F. J., Sharp, L., Carsin, A.-E., Kelleher, T., & Comber, H. (2008). Questionnaire order significantly increased response to a postal survey sent to primary care physicians. *Journal of Clinical Epidemiology, 61*(2), 177–185. https://doi.org/10.1016/j.jclinepi.2007.04.012

Edgar, K., Martin, C., & O'Donnell, I. (2003). *Prison violence: The dynamics of conflict, fear and power*: Willan.

Ericsson, K. A., & Simon, H. A. (1980). Verbal reports as data. *Psychological Review, 87*(3), 215–251. https://doi.org/10.1037/0033-295X.87.3.215

Gallhofer, I. N., & Saris, W. E. (2007). *Design, evaluation, and analysis of questionnaires for survey research.* Wiley.

Goossens, E., & Daems, T. (2023). Detention monitor (KU Leuven). *Zenodo.* https://doi.org/10.5281/zenodo.10229096

Goossens, E., Maes, E., Robert, L., Daems, T., & Mertens, A. (2023). Victimization in prison. A study of victimization and prison climate dimensions in Belgian prisons. *Victims & Offenders,* 1-35. https://doi.org/10.1080/15564886.2023.2282978

Hensley, C., Koscheski, M., & Tewksbury, R. (2005). Examining the characteristics of male sexual assault targets in a Southern maximum-security prison. *Journal of Interpersonal Violence, 20*(6), 667–679. https://doi.org/10.1177/0886260505276069

Hertzum, M., Hansen, K. D., & Andersen, H. H. K. (2009). Scrutinising usability evaluation: Does thinking aloud affect behaviour and mental workload? *Behaviour and Information Technology, 28*(2), 165–181. https://doi.org/10.1080/01449290701773842

Howard, M. V. A., Corben, S. P., Raudino, A., & Galouzis, J. J. (2020). Maintaining safety in the prison environment: A multilevel analysis of inmate victimisation in assaults. *International Journal of Offender Therapy and Comparative Criminology, 64*(10–11), 1091–1113. https://doi.org/10.1177/0306624X19871633

Ireland, J. L., & Qualter, P. (2008). Bullying and social and emotional loneliness in a sample of adult male prisoners. *International Journal of Law and Psychiatry, 31*(1), 19–29. https://doi.org/10.1016/j.ijlp.2007.11.005

Israel, M. (2015). *Research ethics and integrity for social scientists: Beyond regulatory compliance.* SAGE.

Ji, X., & Rau, P.-L.P. (2019). A comparison of three think-aloud protocols used to evaluate a voice intelligent agent that expresses emotions. *Behaviour and Information Technology, 38*(4), 375–383. https://doi.org/10.1080/0144929X.2018.1535621

Jones, T. R., & Pratt, T. C. (2008). The prevalence of sexual violence in prison: The state of the knowledge base and implications for evidence-based correctional policy making. *International Journal of Offender Therapy and Comparative Criminology, 52*(3), 280–295. https://doi.org/10.1177/0306624X07307631

Klatt, T., & Kliem, S. (2021). The influence of harsh parenting and parental warmth during childhood on later involvement in prison misconduct. *Journal of Interpersonal Violence, 36*(13–14), 6838–6858. https://doi.org/10.1177/0886260518820675

Kjellsson, G., Clarke, P., & Gerdtham, U.-G. (2014). Forgetting to remember or remembering to forget: A study of the recall period length in health care survey questions. *Journal of Health Economics, 35*(1), 34–46. https://doi.org/10.1016/j.jhealeco.2014.01.007

Krosnich, J. A. (2018). Improving question design to maximize reliability and validity. In D. L. Vannette & J. A. Krosnick (Eds.), *The Palgrave Handbook of Survey Research* (pp. 95–101). Springer International Publishing. https://doi.org/10.1007/978-3-319-54395-6

Kuo, S.-Y. (2019). Prison victimization among Taiwanese male inmates: An application of importation, deprivation, and routine activities theories. *Security Journal, 33*(4), 602–621. https://doi.org/10.1057/s41284-019-00202-9

Kuo, S.-Y., Chang, K., Chen, Y., & Lai, Y. (2021). Assessing the victim-offender overlap in prison victimization and misconduct among Taiwanese male inmates. *British Journal of Criminology, 20*, 1–22. https://doi.org/10.1093/bjc/azab066

Kuo, S-Y., Cuvelier, S. J., & Huang, Y. (2014). Identifying risk factors for victimization among male prisoners in Taiwan. *International Journal of Offender Therapy and Comparative Criminology, 58*(2), 231–257. https://doi.org/10.1177/0306624X12465272

Lavrakas, P. J. (2008). *Encyclopedia of Survey Research Methods*. Sage.

Listwan, S. J., Daigle, L. E., Hartman, J. L., & Guastaferro, W. P. (2014). Poly-victimization risk in prison: The influence of individual and institutional factors. *Journal of Interpersonal Violence, 29*(13), 2458–2481. https://doi.org/10.1177/0886260513518435

Lee, R. M. (1999). *Doing research on sensitive topics*. Sage.

Lynch, J. P., & Addington, L. A. (2010). Identifying and addressing response errors in self-report surveys. In A. R. Piquero & D. Weisburd (Eds.), *Handbook of Quantitative Criminology* (pp. 251–272). Springer-Verlag.

Martens, S., van Ginneken, E. F. J. C., & Palmen, H. (2021). Slachtofferschap en slachtoffer-daderschap in Nederlandse penitentiaire inrichtingen. *Tijdschrift voor Criminologie*, 399–422.

McGrath, S. A., Marcum, C. D., & Copes, H. (2012). The effects of experienced, vicarious, and anticipated strain on violence and drug use among inmates. *American Journal of Criminal Justice, 37*(1), 60–75. https://doi.org/10.1007/s12103-011-9127-1

McNeeley, S. (2022). Reaffirming the relationship between routine activities and violent victimization in prison. *Journal of Criminal Justice, 78*, 1–11. https://doi.org/10.1016/j.jcrimjus.2022.101883

Moser, D. J., Arndt, S., Kanz, J. E., Benjamin, M. L., Bayless, J. D., Reese, R. L., Paulsen, J. S., & Flaum, M. A. (2004). Coercion and informed consent in research involving prisoners. *Comprehensive Psychiatry, 45*(1), 1–9. https://doi.org/10.1016/j.comppsych.2003.09.009

Meade, B., Wasileski, G., & Hunter, A. (2021). The effects of victimization prior to prison on victimization, misconduct, and sanction severity during incarceration. *Crime and Delinquency, 67*(12), 1856–1878. https://doi.org/10.1177/0011128720977440

Muehlenhard, C. L., Peterson, Z. D., Humphreys, T. P., & Jozkowski, K. N. (2017). Evaluating the one-in-five statistic: Women's risk of sexual assault while in college. *The Journal of Sex Research, 54*(4–5), 549–576. https://doi.org/10.1080/00224499.2017.1295014

Neubacher, F. (2020). On the development, origins and manifestations of prison violence –Evidence from a longitudinal study on young males and females in Germany. *Kriminologie—Das Online-Journal, 3*, 372–393. https://doi.org/10.18716/ojs/krimoj/2020.3.1

Olmsted-Hawala, E., Murphy, E., Hawala, S., & Ashenfelter, K. (2010). Think-aloud protocols: A comparison of three think-aloud protocols for use in testing data-dissemination web sites for usability. *Conference on Human Factors in Computing Systems—Proceedings, 4*, 2381–2390. https://doi.org/10.1145/1753326.1753685

Ramirez, I. L., & Straus, M. A. (2006). The effect of question order on disclosure of intimate partner violence: An experimental test using the conflict tactics scales. *Journal of Family Violence, 21*(1), 1–9. https://doi.org/10.1007/s10896-005-9000-4

Reyns, B. W., Woo, Y., Lee, H. D., & Yoon, O.-K. (2018). Vulnerability versus opportunity: Dissecting the role of low self-control and risky lifestyles in violent victimization risk among Korean inmates. *Crime & Delinquency, 64*(4), 423–447. https://doi.org/10.1177/0011128716679375

Rocconi, L. M., Dumford, A. D., & Butler, B. (2020). Examining the meaning of vague quantifiers in higher education: How often is "often"? *Research in Higher Education, 61*(2), 229–247. https://doi.org/10.1007/s11162-020-09587-8

Roffee, J. A., & Waling, A. (2017). Resolving ethical challenges when researching with minority and vulnerable populations: LGBTIQ victims of violence, harassment and bullying. *Research Ethics Review, 13*(1), 4–22. https://doi.org/10.1177/1747016116658693

Rufino, K. A., Fox, K. A., Cramer, R. J., & Kercher, G. A. (2013). The gang–victimization link: Considering the effects of ethnicity and protective behaviors among prison inmates. *Deviant Behavior, 34*(1), 25–37. https://doi.org/10.1080/01639625.2012.679898

Schwarz, N. (1999). Self-reports: How the questions shape the answers. *The American Psychologist, 54*(2), 93–105. https://doi.org/10.1037/0003-066X.54.2.93

Straus, M., Hamby, S. L., Boney-McCoy, S., & Sugarman, D. B. (1996). The Revised Conflict Tactics Scales (CTS2): Development and preliminary psychometric data. *Journal of Family Issues, 17*(3), 283–316. https://doi.org/10.1177/019251396017003001

Sykes, G. M. (1958). *The society of captives: A study of a maximum security prison*. Princeton University Press.

Teclaw, R., Price, M. C., & Osatuke, K. (2012). Demographic question placement: Effect on item response rates and means of a veterans health administration survey. *Journal of Business and Psychology, 27*(3), 281–290. https://doi.org/10.1007/s10869-011-9249-y

Toman, E. L. (2019). The victim-offender overlap behind bars: Linking prison misconduct and victimization. *Justice Quarterly, 36*(2), 350–382. https://doi.org/10.1080/07418825.2017.1402072

Tourangeau, R., Rips, L. J., & Rasinski, K. A. (2000). *The psychology of survey response*. Cambridge University Press.

Trenor, J. P., Miller, M. K., & Gipson, K. (2011). *Utilization of a think-aloud protocol to cognitively validate a survey instrument identifying social capital resources of engineering undergraduates*. American Society of Engineering

Education Annual Conference and Exhibition. https://peer.asee.org/utilization-of-a-think-aloud-protocol-to-cognitively-validate-a-survey-instrument-identifying-social-capital-resources-of-engineering-undergraduates

van Ginneken, E. F. J. C., Palmen, H., Bosma, A. Q., Nieuwbeerta, P., & Berghuis, M. L. (2018). The Life in Custody Study: The quality of prison life in Dutch prison regimes. *Journal of Criminological Research, Policy and Practice, 4*(4), 253–268. https://doi.org/10.1108/JCRPP-07-2018-0020

Vertommen, T., Schipper-van Veldhoven, N., Wouters, K., Kampen, J. K., Brackenridge, C. H., Rhind, D. J. A., Neels, K., & Van Den Eede, F. (2016). Interpersonal violence against children in sport in the Netherlands and Belgium. *Child Abuse & Neglect, 51,* 223–236. https://doi.org/10.1016/j.chiabu.2015.10.006

Walentynowicz, M., Schneider, S., Junghaenel, D. U., & Stone, A. A. (2022). Vague quantifiers demonstrate little susceptibility to frame of reference effects. *Applied Research in Quality of Life, 17*(1), 317–331. https://doi.org/10.1007/s11482-020-09889-0

Wänke, M. (2002). Conversational norms and the interpretation of vague quantifiers. *Applied Cognitive Psychology, 16*(3), 301–307. https://doi.org/10.1002/acp.787

Warren, J. I., & Jackson, S. L. (2012). *Risk markers for sexual victimization and predation in prison.* Taylor and Francis.

Wilkinson, J., & Fleming, J. (2021). Prisoner-on-prisoner drug searches in prisons in England and Wales: "Business as usual." *Incarceration, 2*(2), 1–17. https://doi.org/10.1177/26326663211015852

Wolff, N., Aizpurua, E., & Peng, D. (2022). Violence against incarcerated women: Predicting risk through the lens of childhood harm. *Violence against Women, 28*(10), 2466–2492. https://doi.org/10.1177/10778012211035814

Wolff, N., Blitz, C. L., Shi, J., Bachman, R., & Siegel, J. A. (2006). Sexual violence inside prisons: Rates of victimization. *Journal of Urban Health, 83*(5), 835–848. https://doi.org/10.1007/s11524-006-9065-2

Wolff, N., Blitz, C. L., Shi, J., Siegel, J., & Bachman, R. (2007). Physical violence inside prisons: Rates of victimization. *Criminal Justice and Behavior, 34*(5), 588–599. https://doi.org/10.1177/0093854806296830

Wolff, N., & Shi, J. (2009a). Feelings of safety among male inmates: The safety paradox. *Criminal Justice Review, 34*(3), 404–427. https://doi.org/10.1177/0734016809333343

Wolff, N., & Shi, J. (2009b). Type, source, and patterns of physical victimization: A comparison of male and female inmates. *The Prison Journal, 89*(2), 172–191. https://doi.org/10.1177/0032885509334754

Wolff, N., Shi, J., & Bachman, R. (2008). Measuring victimization inside prisons: Questioning the questions. *Journal of Interpersonal Violence, 23*(10), 1343–1362. https://doi.org/10.1177/0886260508314301

Wood, S. R., & Buttaro, A. (2013). Co-occurring severe mental illnesses and substance abuse disorders as predictors of state prison inmate assaults. *Crime & Delinquency, 59*(4), 510–535. https://doi.org/10.1177/001112871 2470318

Wooldredge, J., & Steiner, B. (2013). Violent victimization among state prison inmates. *Violence and victims, 28*(3), 531–551. https://doi.org/10.1891/0886-6708.11-00141

Wooldredge, J., & Steiner, B. (2014). A bi-level framework for understanding prisoner victimization. *Journal of Quantitative Criminology, 30*(1), 141–162. https://doi.org/10.1007/s10940-013-9197-y

Wright, D. B., Gaskell, G. D., & O'Muircheartaigh, C. A. (1994). How much is 'quite a bit'? Mapping between numerical values and vague quantifiers. *Applied Cognitive Psychology, 8*(5), 479–496. https://doi.org/10.1002/acp.2350080506

Wright, D. B., Wolff, S. M., Jaspal, R., Barnett, J., & Breakwell, G. M. (2022). The choice of response alternatives in COVID-19 social science surveys. *Public Library of Science (PLoS), 17*(11), 1–17. https://doi.org/10.1371/journal.pone.0263552

Zhao, T., & McDonald, S. (2010). *Keep talking: An analysis of participant utterances gathered using two concurrent think-aloud methods.* NordiCHI 2010: Extending Boundaries - Proceedings of the 6th Nordic Conference on Human-Computer Interaction, 581–590. https://doi.org/10.1145/1868914.1868979

Independent Monitoring and Victimisation in Prisons

Tom Daems

1 Introduction

How can we get a fair picture of victimisation in prisons? It seems to be impossible to provide a clear-cut answer to that question. It depends, first of all, on how victimisation is defined, as Elien Goossens and Aurore Vanliefde highlight in their chapters in this volume (Goossens, 2024; Vanliefde, 2024). Moreover, different methods tend to produce different images of victimisation. We can rely on data that are readily available to us, that is, data produced by the criminal justice system itself: the chapter by Jo Wilkinson offers us a splendid example (Wilkinson, 2024). Or we can produce our own data, for example by designing our own measuring instruments (such as victim surveys) and collecting data directly in prisons (Goossens & Daems, 2024) or by using a qualitative approach and asking actors, such as prison governors, about their experiences with victimisation in prisons (van Ginneken, 2024). And

---

T. Daems (✉)
Leuven Institute of Criminology (LINC), KU Leuven, Leuven, Belgium
e-mail: tom.daems@kuleuven.be

obviously, there are many other ways: studying medical records or disciplinary reports, for example, or interviewing prisoners directly about their experiences. Such questions on measurement methods and on ways to shed light on the 'dark figure' (that is, victims' experiences that tend to remain hidden from view) are not new, of course: they have haunted criminology since its early inception, from the moral statistics of Guerry and Quételet in the nineteenth century to the development of self-report and victim surveys in the second half of the twentieth century.

In this final chapter we would like to explore, briefly and tentatively, what independent monitoring bodies could contribute to our understanding of prison victimisation. Prison monitoring bodies are not designed for scientific or measuring purposes; indeed, they have their own objectives, that is, they play a key role in preventing torture and inhuman or degrading treatment or punishment. However, as part of their preventive mandate, such bodies tend to have unlimited access to prisons: monitors can use their eyes, noses and ears to sense what happens in prisons; they can talk, in private, to prisoners and staff; and they usually have access to written documents, such as medical and disciplinary records, which may give them a unique opportunity to paint a picture of victimisation in the prisons they visit. The facilities offered to such bodies, as well as their recent proliferation throughout Europe (and beyond), may therefore offer further, largely unexplored, possibilities to understand and address victimisation in prisons.

2 Independent Prison Monitoring: Historical Origins and Current State of Affairs

The practice of persons external to the prison system visiting and inspecting such institutions has a long history. The most well-known example, perhaps, is John Howard, who visited penitentiary institutions in different parts of Europe. In his famous book *The State of the Prisons* Howard documented and elaborated at length on his observations and impressions from his many visits. Interestingly, when John

Howard visited the famous octagon in Ghent in the late eighteenth century, he explicitly referred to the 'excellent rules for preventing all quarreling' in the institution (Howard, 1777: 144). These kinds of visits have been common throughout the history of the modern prison. It is only recently, however, that independent prison monitoring became an organised, systematic practice, oriented towards a well-defined goal, that is, the prevention of torture and inhuman or degrading treatment or punishment.

For the origins of prison monitoring, as part of such a broader human rights infrastructure, we need to return to the early 1970s. In 1973 Amnesty International, as part of a global campaign it had launched one year earlier, published its *Report on Torture*. Here Amnesty painted a rather bleak picture about torture. Indeed, almost three decades after the end of World War II, and notwithstanding a number of important global and regional developments aimed at strengthening the protection of human rights, Amnesty came to the conclusion that '…the use of torture has by all indications increased over the last few years' (Amnesty International, 1973: 17). It is against that background that we can observe an increasing mobilisation on this topic, from the mid-1970s onwards, in particular at the level of the UN, with the 1975 UN Declaration against Torture and the start of negotiations for what later (in 1984) became the UN Convention against Torture (on this, see, e.g., Rodley, 2009).

However, at the same time some started to question the legal-judicial approach to fighting torture. Jean-Jacques Gautier, inspired by the International Committee of the Red Cross, which visits places of detention in situations of war or conflict, suggested that a similar visiting mechanism might be useful and feasible in peace time. In 1976 Gautier outlined in *La vie protestante* the basic rationale of what came to be referred to as 'a new weapon in the fight against torture' (Gautier, 1976). The proposal focused on a system of routine visits, mutual assistance and collaboration, prevention and the possibility of swift action. It was believed that such a preventive mechanism, based on visits, would be more effective than a rather dramatic, time-consuming, judicial approach (Gautier, 1980: 35).

These ideas reverberate in the hardware and software of contemporary monitoring bodies. Indeed, Art. 1 of the European Convention for the Prevention of Torture and Inhuman or Degrading Treatment or Punishment states that the European Committee for the Prevention of Torture and Inhuman or Degrading Treatment or Punishment (CPT) '…shall, by means of visits, examine the treatment of persons deprived of their liberty with a view to strengthening, if necessary, the protection of such persons from torture and from inhuman or degrading treatment or punishment'. To carry out its task states provide the CPT with a number of facilities, as listed in Art. 8: 'access to its territory and the right to travel without restriction; full information on the places where persons deprived of their liberty are being held; unlimited access to any place where persons are deprived of their liberty, including the right to move inside such places without restriction; other information available to the Party which is necessary for the Committee to carry out its task'. Art. 8 further stipulates that the CPT may interview in private persons deprived of their liberty and may communicate freely with any person whom it believes can supply relevant information. Such facilities are indispensable for the CPT to execute its key task, that is, to gather all sorts of information in situ which is the raw material for the observations and recommendations formulated in CPT reports which, subsequently, feed into the ongoing dialogue (for a further discussion, see Bicknell et al., 2018; Daems, 2017).

Within the UN human rights system, the Optional Protocol to the Convention against Torture and other Cruel, Inhuman or Degrading Treatment or Punishment (OPCAT) establishes a similar system, that is, '…a system of regular visits undertaken by independent international and national bodies to places where people are deprived of their liberty, in order to prevent torture and other cruel, inhuman or degrading treatment or punishment' (Art. 1). However, next to establishing an international monitoring body (that is, the Subcommittee on Prevention of Torture and other Cruel, Inhuman or Degrading Treatment or Punishment (SPT)), the OPCAT also requires states to '… set up, designate or maintain at the domestic level one or several visiting bodies for the prevention of torture and other cruel, inhuman or degrading treatment or punishment (hereinafter referred to as the national preventive mechanism)' (art. 3). Both the SPT and these so-called National Preventive

Mechanisms (NPM) visit places of detention '…with a view to strengthening, if necessary, the protection of these persons against torture and other cruel, inhuman or degrading treatment or punishment' (art. 4). For this states need to grant such monitoring bodies facilities with respect to access to places of detention and information as well as possibilities to interview whomever they want in private (Art. 14 and 20, see further Evans, 2023). With the recent addition of the SPT and NPMs to the monitoring landscape in Europe, some have described the relationship between such bodies (CPT-SPT-NPM) as 'triangular', '…linking as it does three mechanisms engaged in preventive visiting across the regional, international and national divides' (Bicknell & Evans, 2017: 16).

3 Methodology

Again, the primary task of such monitoring bodies is not to map or study victimisation patterns. Independent monitoring has been designed from the idea that places of detention often tend to have a total control over those deprived of their liberty and makes detainees therefore vulnerable, given the '…constant conflict between human standards on one hand and institutional efficiency on the other' (Goffman, 1961: 76). The institution's objectives ('institutional efficiency': order, security, forced care) tend to override individual needs and concerns ('humane standards': dignity). For that reason the Dutch penologist Constantijn Kelk once introduced the metaphor of the rubber ball: 'We have to realize that the total institution - like a rubber ball that jumps back after being squeezed - has the tendency to revert to old "natural" properties and patterns over and over again if not continuously and with great alertness from the outside emphasis is placed on the realization of law and legal principles' (Kelk, 1983: 23, translated from Dutch). The facilities offered to such monitoring bodies to execute such a preventive mandate—unlimited access to places of detention, to written documents, to people of flesh and blood—may seem self-evident from today's perspective but such facilities were revolutionary in the early days of the CPT, as its first President, Antonio Cassese recalled: 'Never, in the history of international affairs, had a multinational group of persons—independent of governmental control—been granted formal authority to penetrate the *sancta sanctorum* of each state (police stations, prisons, psychiatric hospitals, etc.), in other words those very places where national sovereignty is given its overpowering yet most recondite expression' (Cassese, 1996: 1). And, indeed, it is still not that evident today, as the SPT highlights in its twelfth annual report ('too many States parties appear to have resiled from their enthusiasm and commitment to torture prevention, by challenging the mandate of the Subcommittee and not establishing and supporting national preventive mechanisms as the Optional Protocol envisages' (SPT, 2019: 10)) and, in fact, as it experienced recently, when a visit to Australia was suspended (on 23 October 2022) due to the lack of cooperation of Australia (SPT, 2022).

This revolutionary character of the facilities offered to such monitoring bodies may, intuitively at least, appeal to prison researchers. Indeed, also prison researchers need access to institutions, to archival documents and/or to people. Obtaining formal permissions, getting access, building trust, establishing rapport, …: for many this implies time-consuming paper-work, phone calls, meetings, small-talk and living with many uncertainties (Will permission from the central prison administration be granted? How will local prison governors and prison staff react? What about ethics and data management protocols and approvals? What will be the quality of the records kept in the prisons? What if a virus (let's say COVID-19) jeopardises data collection within the set time-frame of the project?). For a monitoring body such obstacles are non-existent: indeed, it is part of the DNA of independent monitoring that unlimited access is granted, unconditionally. There are, of course, some possible limits in terms of access (e.g. Art. 14.2 OPCAT stipulates that a visit to a particular place of detention can be objected to but '…only on urgent and compelling grounds of national defence, public safety, natural disaster or serious disorder in the place to be visited that temporarily prevent the carrying out of such a visit'; see also Art. 9.1 ECPT) and the information gathered by monitoring bodies, as well as its reports, is in principle confidential, unless states grant permission to publish the reports. However, in Europe at least, most reports of the CPT have been published on its website and a large number of countries (so far, fifteen) have even agreed with its 'automatic publication procedure', which implies that all future visit reports concerning those states are made public immediately.[1]

The facilities that monitoring bodies have in terms of access and data gathering have also attracted the attention of prison researchers. Jefferson and Martin (2023: 26) recently argued that '…prison ethnographers and prison monitors have more in common than typically imagined or admitted'. And they suggested '…that ongoing exploration of the complementarity of different "styles of external scrutiny" might enable scrutinizers to scrutinize prisons more reflexively' (Jefferson & Martin, 2023: 26). Moreover, prison monitoring has some obvious parallels with 'prison tourism' or 'carceral tours' (Vander Beken, 2017) which also could be further explored in future research and debate on victimisation in prisons.

References

Amnesty International. (1973). *Report on Torture*. Duckworth.

Bicknell, C., & Evans, M. (2017). Monitoring prisons: The increasingly complex relationship between international and domestic frameworks. In T. Daems & L. Robert (Eds.), *Europe in prisons* (pp. 11–35). Palgrave Macmillan.

Bicknell, C., Evans, M., & Morgan, R. (2018). *Preventing torture in Europe*. Council of Europe.

Cassese, A. (1996). *Inhuman states. Imprisonment, detention and torture in Europe today*. Polity Press.

Daems, T. (2017). Slaves and statues: Torture prevention in contemporary Europe. *British Journal of Criminology*, 57(3), 627–643, https://doi.org/10.1093/bjc/azv133

Evans, M. D. (2023). *Tackling torture: Prevention in practice*. Bristol University Press.

---

[1] At the time of writing (17.12.23) these were: Albania, Austria, Bulgaria, the Czech Republic, Denmark, Finland, Lithuania, Luxembourg, the Republic of Moldova, Monaco, North Macedonia, Norway, Slovenia, Sweden and Ukraine (URL: https://www.coe.int/en/web/cpt/faqs#automatic-procedure).

Gautier, J.-J. (1976). La proposition de Jean-Jacques Gautier. In N. Mischler (Ed.), *Jean-Jacques Gautier et la prévention de la torture: de l'idée à l'action. Recueil de textes* (pp. 229–232). L'Association pour la prévention de la torture.

Gautier, J.-J. (1980). The case for an effective and realistic procedure. In International Commission of Jurists & Swiss Committee Against Torture (Eds.), *Torture: How to make the International Convention effective. A draft Optional Protocol* (pp. 31–38). International Commission of Jurists.

Goffman, E. (1961). *Asylums: Essays on the social situation of mental patients and other inmates*. Penguin.

Goossens, E. (2024). Methodological challenges to victimisation studies. In T. Daems, & E. Goossens (Eds.), *Understanding Prisoner Victimisation*. Palgrave Macmillan.

Goossens, E., & Daems, T. (2024). Mapping and explaining victimisation among prisoners in Flanders. In T. Daems, & E. Goossens (Eds.), *Understanding Prisoner Victimisation*. Palgrave Macmillan.

Howard, J. (1777). *The State of the Prisons in England and Wales with Preliminary Observations and an Account of Some Foreign Prisons*. William Eyres.

Jefferson, A. M., & Martin, T. M. (2023). Monitors and ethnographers: A reflection on affinities and potential synergies. *Prison Service Journal, 265*, 26–34.

Kelk, C. (1983). *Recht voor geïnstitutionaliseerden*. Gouda Quint.

Rodley, N. (2009). *The treatment of prisoners under international law*. Oxford University Press.

SPT. (2019, March 13). *Twelfth annual report of the Subcommittee on Prevention of Torture and Other Cruel, Inhuman or Degrading Treatment or Punishment*. CAT/C/66/2.

SPT. (2022, October 23). UN torture prevention body suspends visit to Australia citing lack of co-operation. https://www.ohchr.org/en/press-rel eases/2022/10/un-torture-prevention-body-suspends-visit-australia-citing-lack-co-operation

Vander Beken, T. (2017). Learning from carceral tours: Reflections after a Howard tour across Europe. In T. Daems & L. Robert (Eds.), *Europe in prisons* (pp. 79–101). Palgrave Macmillan.

Van Ginneken, E. F. J. C. (2024). The victim-offender overlap in prisons and associated challenges for prison managers. In T. Daems, & E. Goossens (Eds.), *Understanding Prisoner Victimisation*. Palgrave Macmillan.

Vanliefde, A. (2024). Vulnerability and victimhood in prison: Reflecting on the concept of vulnerability in prisoner victimisation research. In T. Daems, & E. Goossens (Eds.), *Understanding Prisoner Victimisation*. Palgrave Macmillan.

Wilkinson, J. (2024). Who's who? Individual characteristics of those involved in sexual assaults in adult men's prisons in England and Wales. In T. Daems, & E. Goossens (Eds.), *Understanding Prisoner Victimisation*. Palgrave Macmillan.

Index

A
Aggression 3, 5, 23, 95, 103, 125
Antagonism 50, 52, 53, 58, 69, 71, 79, 80, 93
Architecture 64, 125
Assault 5, 13–15, 18–23, 25–33, 35, 36, 38–41, 52, 57, 89–92, 94–96, 104, 109, 145, 147

C
Consequences 5, 16, 52, 99, 118, 120, 128
Contraband 5, 17, 22, 26, 27, 39, 89, 91, 92, 94, 97, 98, 102, 103, 106, 107
Control 3, 6, 50, 51, 60, 71, 82, 92, 95, 99, 100, 107, 109, 125, 179, 180
Correctional officers 4

D
Drugs 18, 24, 26, 27, 40, 93, 95, 96, 98–102, 104, 107–109

E
Emotional victimisation (EV) 53, 57, 62–64, 68–77, 79
threats, threatening 7, 28, 77, 90, 157
European Committee for the Prevention of Torture and Inhuman or Degrading Treatment or Punishment (CPT) 2, 54, 178–180
European Court of Human Rights (ECtHR) 2, 117, 118, 121–123, 127
EU 2020–2025 Strategy on victims' rights 122

Index

G

Guardianship 6, 50, 51, 58, 60, 69–71, 78, 92

H

Human rights 3, 7, 8, 115–118, 123, 149, 177, 178

I

Institutional victimisation 124
Irwin & Cressey 50, 91
    importation theory 91

L

Lesbian, gay, bisexual, transgender, queer, intersex (LGBTQI+) 38, 123–125, 132
Lifestyle 6, 50, 51, 53, 58, 60, 69, 71, 74, 75, 79, 80, 93, 107

M

Material victimisation (MV) 52, 53, 57, 60, 62, 64, 65, 68–74, 76–79, 81
Mental health 5, 52, 55, 119, 123
    mental illness, disability, disorder 4, 50, 52, 91, 123

P

Physical victimisation (PV) 52, 53, 57, 61, 62, 66, 68–81, 145, 147–150, 154, 163
    fights, fighting 52, 58, 78, 90, 92, 94, 101, 147, 177

Prison climate 105, 125, 134, 159
Prison environment 16, 59, 125
Prison Rape Elimination Act (PREA) 2, 13, 23, 40
Prison staff 3, 4, 14, 15, 20, 21, 23, 41, 51, 120, 123, 125, 132, 133, 135, 158, 159, 161, 164, 180
Psychological victimisation 150

R

Risk factors 3, 4, 6, 7, 23, 49, 52, 60, 77, 78, 81, 82, 91, 92, 147, 149, 150
    contextual characteristics, factors, variables 64, 79, 82, 119–121, 124, 134
    individual characteristics 6, 14, 19–21, 27, 39, 119, 121, 126
Routine-activity theory 92

S

Safety, feelings of safety 7, 40, 41, 96–98, 100, 106, 107, 109, 120, 125, 132, 133, 158
Security, security level 19, 23, 25, 27, 82, 91, 93, 105, 179
Sex offender 5, 27, 30, 51, 71
Sexual victimisation (SV) 5, 13, 14, 17–19, 23, 24, 27, 32, 34–39, 49, 52, 53, 56–58, 62, 67–80, 145, 146, 148, 153, 163
    rape 5, 13, 17, 36, 148
    sexual assault, aggression 2, 5, 13–15, 17, 18, 24, 31, 33, 36, 39

Social control-opportunity theory 92, 93
Survey 8, 36, 39, 49, 56, 78, 93, 94, 145, 147, 148, 151, 154, 156, 157, 159, 160, 164, 175, 176
Sykes, G.M. 16, 17, 23, 50, 51, 91, 96, 149
  deprivation theory 91, 107
  pains of imprisonment 16, 24, 91, 96

V
Verbal 3, 22, 28, 30, 35, 56, 94, 146, 148, 151, 160, 161
Victim-offender overlap 6, 51, 77, 78, 81, 90–94, 96
Violence 1–6, 8, 24, 28, 30, 31, 36, 40, 50, 52, 61, 62, 70, 73, 79, 80, 90, 94, 97, 101, 103, 116, 125, 130, 133, 146–148, 153, 154, 157
Vulnerability 7, 22, 23, 36, 50, 52, 53, 55, 57, 59, 60, 69, 72, 79, 80, 91, 93, 94, 115–135

Printed by Printforce, United Kingdom